W9-AAV-888

TONY HINKLE

TONY HINKLE

Coach for All Seasons

Howard Caldwell

Indiana University Press
BLOOMINGTON AND INDIANAPOLIS

The paper used in this publication meets the minimum requirements of American National Standard for Information Sciences—Permanence of Paper for Printed Library Materials, ANSI Z39.48-1984.

Manufactured in the United States of America

Library of Congress Cataloging-in-Publication Data

Caldwell, Howard, date.
Tony Hinkle : a coach for all seasons / Howard Caldwell.
p. cm.
Includes bibliographical references and index.
ISBN 0-253-31298-1 (alk. paper)
1. Hinkle, Tony. 2. Football—United States—Coaches—Biography. 3. Basketball—United States—Coaches—Biography. 4. Butler University—Football—History. 5. Butler University—Basketball—History. I. Title.
GV939.H525C35 1991
796.332'092—dc20

[B] 90-49194

1 2 3 4 5 95 94 93 92 91

To the coach and his kids—
those who starred on his teams
and those who didn't
but gave him their best

CONTENTS

FOREWORD
by Bob Knight

Tony Hinkle may well be the most remarkable coach in American collegiate athletic history. Certainly no man has been involved with more athletes in more sports over a longer period of time than he. When one thinks of great coaches, classifications are made by sports: in basketball, Pete Newell, Clair Bee, Joe Lapchik, Red Auerbach, and Fred Taylor; in football, Bo Schembechler, Joe Paterno, Bear Bryant, Darrell Royal, and Jock Sutherland. None of the great names in college coaching are thought of as two-, much less three-, sport coaches, with the exception of Tony Hinkle. He was as good as any of them in both football and basketball. In addition, he did an outstanding job with his baseball teams. Tony himself was a great athlete at the University of Chicago and played with another of the legendary athletes of his time and later a great contributor to college football as a coach at Minnesota, Princeton, and Michigan: Fritz Crisler. Tony's story is not just that of a man devoted to providing a lot of boys with a way to become successful men, it is in itself a unique history of the development of intercollegiate athletics. Because of all the championships his teams won, all the players whose lives he affected in all the sports that he coached, Tony Hinkle stands alone as The Coach.

Howard Caldwell has done every fan of college athletics a great service in providing this informative and readable biography. As a reporter, Howard has been famous for years for going beyond the headlines to provide clear and accurate accounts of contemporary events. He has brought that same dedication and insight to *Tony Hinkle: Coach for All Seasons*, and we are all in his debt.

PREFACE

Lots of us who grew up in central Indiana were lucky enough to have a family member introduce us to football and basketball at Butler University at a tender age. In my case it was a father who had covered the football games as a student correspondent for the *Indianapolis Sun* prior to World War I.

My guess is that I was introduced to Butler football about the time Tony Hinkle took over the head coaching job in 1934. I became a loyal fan and immediately began keeping records on each and every game. By 1936 my sister had enrolled at Butler and I got caught up in the basketball program, awed by the big-name schools that came to Butler Fieldhouse. My record keeping expanded.

By the late 1930s I was rounding up buddies to go to most home games, courtesy of the city's streetcars and buses. Dad talked about Tony as if he were a friend, though he didn't really know him. Tony was a man Dad admired because he conducted himself properly and won more games than he lost. For me, Tony was someone special whom I never expected to meet, let alone write about someday. He was the man in charge down on the field or on the court, intent on producing another win for my father and mother and sister's alma mater.

As a journalism major at Butler after service in World War II, I became sports editor of the school newspaper, the *Collegian*, which was published four times a week in those days. Now I could wax poetic about the school and coach I had followed so long. Later, as a broadcaster in Terre Haute, I moved for a time into covering basketball play by play, describing games at Butler Fieldhouse when Indiana State came to call and during two historic Indiana High School Athletic Association basketball tournaments. The first one was in 1954 when little Milan, coached by a Hinkle graduate, upset Muncie Central, and the second was in 1955 when Crispus Attucks, led by Oscar Robertson, became the first Indianapolis school to win a state title.

In the 1960s, back in Indianapolis, going to Butler basketball games became a regular activity for my wife and me and our three daughters. Tony produced joy and excitement and entertainment for three generations of my family—one of many, many families who shared the same experience.

All these years later it seemed high time that Tony and his Butler story should be set down for the record. I hope readers find it half as joyful as it was for me.

ACKNOWLEDGMENTS

It was most important to me to have the support and cooperation of Butler University in this endeavor. They were provided most enthusiastically by Butler President Geoffrey Bannister. Day-to-day assistance came from university staff members, who always found the time to answer queries and make suggestions. They include Jim Shaffer, Bill Sylvester, Chris Theofanis, Bob Stalcup, Chris Denari, and Gisela Terrell.

Hinkle family members also were most helpful in granting a series of interviews and in digging out pictures, letters, audio tapes, and other memorabilia that were most valuable to the effort. This help came from Tony's two daughters, Mrs. David Watson (Patty) and Mrs. David Causey (Barbara), and Tony's two sisters, Florence Lord and Lois Hinkle. Close friends and associates also were vital to the project, and this list includes Bob Nipper, Bill Shover, William Powell, Dr. Robert Parr, James Phillippe, Tom Carnegie, Bob Dietz, Bill Hardy, and Herb Schwomeyer.

Help also came from some of the people who covered Tony's many games for newspapers at various times in his career. Thanks goes to Wayne Fuson of the *Indianapolis News* and Bob Collins and John Bansch of the *Indianapolis Star.* In addition, Lawrence Conner of the *Indianapolis Star* allowed me to look through the Star-News photo files for picture prospects. Bob Hammel, long-time sports editor of the *Herald-Times* in Bloomington, contributed to the editing and was most helpful in providing historic sports background. Others who contributed to this story through interviews were Coach Bob Knight, Leo Barnhorst, Dr. Joseph Nygaard, and Coach John Wooden. Hubert Leslie of Logansport was most helpful in running down data on Tony's family of an earlier time. I also wish to thank the University of Chicago Library personnel for providing me access to yearbooks and other data. The staff at Calumet High School (which still exists, though in a different building) were most helpful in finding a yearbook from Tony's school days there.

The following is a list of Butler athletes who were interviewed in the course of research (excluding those previously mentioned): Frank Baird, Don Benbow, Jeff Blue, Ed Bopp, Bill Bugg, Orvis Burdsall, Scott Chandler, Ralph Chapman, Pembroke Cornelius, Wally Cox, Jerry Cranny, William Davis, Joe Dezelan, Jimmy Doyle, Dick Dullaghan, Guy Fish, Ken Freeman, George Freyn, Paul Furnish, Keith Greve, Steve Gross, Bob Hamilton, Tom Harding, Dick Haslam, Jim Hauss, Frank Heddon, Ken Keltner, Dave Konold, Mike McGinley, Lance Middlekauff, Paul Moore, Ralph O'Brien, Ken Pennington, Jerry Petty, Bob Plump, Joe Purichia, Larry Ramey, Dick Reed, Cleon Reynolds, John Riddle, Ed Schilling, Max Schumacher, Larry Shade, Bill Shepherd, Jr., Larry Shook, Tom Sleet, Jerry Steiner, Kent Stewart, Dr. Frank Teague, Bob Wakefield, Norman Williams, Marvin Wood.

My research debts are many. Books I found helpful include Dave Anderson, *The Story of Football* (New York: William Morrow, 1985); Bob Hill and Randall Baron, *The Amazing Basketball Book: The First 100 Years* (Louisville: Full Court Press, 1988); Leo Litz, *Report from the Pacific* (issued by Indianapolis News, 1946); Herb Schwomeyer, *Hoosier Hysteria,* 6th ed. (Greenfield, Ind.: Mitchell-Fleming, 1985); Kenneth L. (Tug) Wilson and Jerry Brondfield, *The Big Ten* (Englewood Cliffs, N.J.: Prentice-Hall, 1967); and John Wooden (as told to Jack Tobin), *They Call Me Coach* (Waco, Tex.: Word Books, 1972).

Butler University publications and records consulted include the *Butler Alumnus* (Wayne Fuson, "The Legend of Paul D. 'Tony' Hinkle," Winter 1966); the *Butler Collegian* student newspaper (selected issues 1921–70); the *Drift* student yearbook (1921–

70); and the Butler Athletic Record Book (1887–1927, 1927–48, and 1948–70).

From the *Indianapolis News* (selected issues 1921–90) I consulted articles by William Fox, Jr., Angelo Angelopolous, Wayne Fuson, Dick Denny, Corky Lamm, Ray Marquette, Dick Mittman, and Lyle Mannweiler; from the *Indianapolis Star* for the same period, articles by Bob Collins, Jep Cadou, Jr., Max Stultz, John Bansch, Max Greenwald, Tom Keating, Harrison Howard, Joe Hamelin, and Mike Chappell; and from the *Indianapolis Times* (selected issues 1921–65), articles by Eddie Ash, Jr., and Dick Mittman. Also consulted was Tom Keating's "The Game the Irish Would Like to Forget," which appeared in the *Star*'s Sunday magazine (November 22, 1981).

For Tony Hinkle's Chicago school days I used the Calumet High School yearbook for 1916 and *Cap and Gown* (1917–21), the University of Chicago student yearbook. I gleaned information about Hinkle's navy days from "Lieut. Hinkle Finding It Tough to Fit 'Kids' Out of School and Pros into Working Team," by Tommy Devine (*Chicago Tribune,* October 30, 1942), and from a Great Lakes Naval Training Center basketball brochure (1942–43) and souvenir football programs (the Notre Dame contests of 1942 and 1943).

I also consulted athletic brochures for 1989–90 from these universities: Notre Dame, Indiana, Purdue, Michigan, Michigan State, Ohio State, Northwestern, Iowa, Wisconsin, Illinois, Evansville, Ball State, Indiana State, St. Joseph's, Valparaiso, Franklin, and Indianapolis.

For providing access to audiotaped interviews with Coach Hinkle conducted by Tom Keating in the early 1980s I wish to thank Bob Collins and Bill Sylvester. Additional thanks goes to Butler University's Instructional Services Center, which transcribed those interviews and many others conducted during the course of the research.

TONY HINKLE

1 Finale with Overture

It was not the kind of moment Tony enjoyed. All these people meant well, he knew that—but being the center of attention was not the sort of thing he ever craved. It made him uncomfortable. It was also unavoidable.

Butler University and thousands of Tony Hinkle's friends were honoring him for all those years he had coached football, basketball, and baseball at the school while also serving as athletic director. They were only a part of what this night was about, however. Butler's fieldhouse, called Hinkle Fieldhouse since 1965, was filled with Tony's "kids." These men knew what it was like to be coached by Tony Hinkle, an experience that had motivated many of them to set higher standards for themselves.

The formal ceremony was taking place before the final basketball game of the season. But it was more than a season's end. It was the last game for the last Butler basketball team Tony would ever coach. It was Monday night, February 23, 1970, and the guest of honor had reached the age of seventy, which school rules said was the maximum age for retirement.

Actually Tony wasn't fully retiring. He was going to remain on the payroll as special assistant to the president of the school,

Alexander Jones. Tony wasn't certain what that title meant except that his office now would be in Jordan Hall, a building about which he knew very little. Tony had taught his classes, on the organization and administration of athletics and on coaching of football and basketball, at the fieldhouse. There was another reason he didn't know much about Jordan Hall. He respected the school's faculty members and had never run interference for any of his "kids" in their classes.

All that part of his life was drawing to a close, somewhat to his amazement. He had concentrated on his busy routine right up to this night and hadn't really thought much about it. His life was centered on preparing for the next opponent and on analyzing what went wrong in the last defeat or what went right in the last win. It was a life that had time for little else, though it was filled with a host of friends, most of them related to the world of athletics, a world that had consumed him, a world that he dearly loved.

Tony probably was startled that night in February as a crowd estimated by the Indianapolis press to be in excess of seventeen thousand rose as one when he appeared for the ceremony he didn't relish. The standing ovation lasted for some two and a half minutes, and it was only the first of several. With him were his daughters, Barbara and Patty, their husbands and children, city and state officials, special friends, and the master of ceremonies, Tom Carnegie, with whom Tony had worked for many years doing telecasts of the Indiana high school basketball tournament games. But anyone who knew Hinkle knew that this ceremony wasn't the coach's idea of pleasure. They also knew that among the thoughts running through that analytical mind of his was one concerning the real reason he was there: to coach a basketball game.

How he loved that game! He had been given his first taste of basketball as a youngster living on the southside of Chicago in the early years of the twentieth century. Hamilton Park wasn't far away, and a park instructor used to let the youngsters who hung out there scrimmage a little after a session of calisthenics. But earlier, young Paul Hinkle had received no encouragement in competitive activities. His early years were consumed with chores on the farm in north central Indiana where he was born. The farm was owned by his mother's parents, and it depended heavily on manpower to survive.

Paul was reaching school age when he and his parents moved to Chicago, but he still spent summers on the farm until the farm was sold about the time he reached high school age. By that time he had found he could compete in baseball, football, and basketball with the many older, rougher youngsters at the park. Athletic competition became a primary interest that could never leave him.

There is no indication that Paul aspired to leadership posts during his high school days, though he participated in four sports: basketball, baseball, golf, and soccer (the school had no football team then). Hinkle also served as secretary of his high school's athletic association.

Not until he went on to the University of Chicago did he receive his first real coaching in football. He earned three varsity letters, playing end. At the time, freshmen were not allowed to play on the varsity level. He moved to the forefront in basketball and baseball even more rapidly, and in leadership positions. He was captain of the baseball team as a freshman and held the same position in basketball his junior and senior years. He earned three letters in each sport and was a basketball all-American his senior year.

Hinkle broadened his activities somewhat at the university. He became a member of Alpha Tau Omega social fraternity and treasurer of the Reynolds Club, comparable to the student union organizations of a later time. But he dated few coeds. In all probability, he felt little confidence in this area of life and was ill at ease among his female classmates. He also operated on a limited budget and was extremely busy with the pressures of starring in college athletics and earning a degree in oil geology.

Hinkle went to Butler University in Indianapolis after graduation when he was offered a coaching job by his former coach at Chicago, Harlan (Pat) Page. The prospect was so attractive that he promptly put aside any thought of pursuing a career in his academic major. From the beginning Butler students were impressed with his savvy as an assistant coach. He had no problem gaining their respect.

Hinkle was a prime example of the self-made athlete-coach, in the sense that he was not pressured or driven by his parents to achieve athletically. His father's ambitions and goals were in teaching; he was aggressive and worked hard at his profession, but he didn't deter his son from moving into an entirely different aspect of education. Yet the standards he maintained in the conduct of the family's life and the attitude he held toward achieving his objectives had a profound effect on Hinkle's conduct.

It wasn't all victories for the young coach at Butler in those early years. At one point he was made athletic director and head football coach, but within a year he had been removed from both positions and replaced by older, more experienced men. When that happened, athletes who played for him said they saw no evidence of change in his demeanor.

Loyalty was a very big part of Tony Hinkle. It grew steadily through the Butler years despite the frustrations that must have come at times from an athletic program at a small private university. Money was a constant limiting factor. He had to reconcile himself to the fact that the school's commitment to football would never equal the commitment to basketball. It would have taken far too much money to bring football up to the same level.

It was an easier matter with basketball in a state that already worshiped the game. When Butler Fieldhouse was opened in 1928 it was like no other basketball facility in the nation, save Madison Square Garden in New York. Hinkle could schedule first-rate teams with relative ease because their coaches wanted to see the fieldhouse and play in it. It also was a magnificent recruiting tool. The best high school teams in Indiana played there in the final games of the annual tournament, and Hinkle was there to welcome them. Combine that with Hinkle's rapid success as a basketball coach and the result was that Butler's schedules came to include some of the most prestigious schools in the country.

Some of that prestige was only a few miles away, up at South Bend, Indiana. Notre Dame was a regular on Hinkle's basketball schedule, at the beginning mostly because of Hinkle's friendship with the man who put Notre Dame on the map as a national football power, Knute Rockne. When Hinkle became head basketball coach at Butler in 1926 he quickly contacted Rockne, who replied in a letter found not long ago in one of Hinkle's cartons of memorabilia:

> I have received your letter and have instructed Mr. Keogan [Notre Dame's basketball coach, George Keogan] to give you two games in basketball next year if he can possibly do so. I told him to get in touch with you directly.
>
> You have a tough job down there, Tony, a job that would appall the average fellow but I believe you will make it.
>
> If there is ever anything I can do to help you—why, feel free to call on me.

Notre Dame didn't get on the schedule that first season, but it did the following season, home and home, and just about every season thereafter during Hinkle's tenure. It was the Irish who provided the opposition when Hinkle's team opened Butler Fieldhouse in 1928, and they did so again in 1970 when Hinkle coached his last team's last game there. As his thousands of fans stood and cheered him that night, Hinkle's thoughts must have been focused at least partly on strategies for coaching his Bulldogs against the Irish.

2 Splinter Hall to Fairview

When the Butler Fieldhouse opener was played in 1928, basketball itself was only in its thirty-seventh year. Appropriately enough, the game was born just seven years before Hinkle, and its birth month was December, the same as Tony's.

Dr. James Naismith invented basketball in December 1891 at Springfield, Massachusetts, now the home of the Naismith Basketball Hall of Fame. First to play it were eighteen men who were preparing to become general secretaries of the YMCA, the Young Men's Christian Association. It happened at the School for Christian Workers, which later became Springfield College. Naismith had joined the faculty there the previous year, along with Amos Alonzo Stagg, who was to play a prominent role in the athletic training of Tony Hinkle.

Naismith was assigned to create something more stimulating than drills with dumbbells and other exercises the men felt were not essential for their training. Members of the school's football team, they had been forced inside by the severe New England weather shortly after the season ended. Naismith struggled, but within weeks he fulfilled the assignment, creating the game that was described in a Hall of Fame pamphlet on the game's history as "what was needed—a recreational game, vigorous enough to attract football men, simple enough so anyone could play it, difficult enough to challenge even the best and interesting and competitive enough to satisfy all and yet safe enough to play inside." The same pamphlet noted that the game "became an instant success in all classes" and was introduced to YMCAs throughout the country.

Just when the first basketball game was played in Indiana is not known. Herb Schwomeyer, in his book *Hoosier Hysteria*, cited a claim by a Crawfordsville newspaper that it occurred at the Crawfordsville YMCA in the spring of 1893. But records at Butler University state that the school had a basketball team in 1892–93, when the institution's first gymnasium was opened. No season record has been found, but twenty-one students are listed as varsity award winners.

What is certain is that football was the major sport at Butler then. Basketball likely was looked on for years as a winter occupation to turn to for conditioning, the basis of its creation. Butler's first gymnasium was too small to provide seating for spectators and in fact provided only minimal services for perspiring performers. The small structure also housed the electrical power system for heat and lights on the campus, then located in Irvington, on the eastside of Indianapolis.

Basketball's popularity grew rapidly throughout Indiana on the high school level. In 1911, when the state had its first high school basketball tournament, crowds stood in line to get a seat to see their hometown schools perform. Butler, in contrast, had to cancel its 1913–14 season because no team would agree to play in its small gym. The following season it played its basketball games on the road. After World War I, when the Officers Training Program was phased out, Butler kept one of two structures the government had built and converted it into a basketball facility, the Winter Garden. For the first time, students could watch their basketball team play.

As the game's popularity grew in the early 1920s, the school turned to a variety of sites in Indianapolis for home games. Students eagerly followed. Tomlinson Hall in downtown Indianapolis was the biggest, with twenty-five hundred seats. It was fine for fans but not always for players, who called it "splinter hall." When Tomlinson wasn't available, scheduling at other sites was necessary. They included the Marion athletic club on North Meridian Street, the YMCA, the Athenaeum, the National Guard Armory, and the Auto Show Building at the State Fairgrounds. Butler didn't get a permanent home for its basketball team until the school moved to Fairview Park on the northside, its present site.

Basketball of the 1920s was far different than it is today. When Tony Hinkle's team met Notre Dame in the 1928 Butler Fieldhouse opener, the center jump was required after every point was scored, a decided advantage to the team with the biggest man. Another such advantage was the absence of the three-second rule. A big man on offense could stand under the basket as long as he wanted to. There also was no time limit for bringing the ball down the floor, and the clock didn't stop running after points were scored, after free throws, or when the ball went out of bounds. These factors help account for the low final scores that were racked up in those days.

Hinkle had a hand in changing the rules. He was a member of the National Rules Committee in the mid-1930s when the center jump rule was removed, and he served on the committee for eight years during the 1940s, two years as its chairman. Hinkle had a good reason for looking out for the little man in basketball. A lot of smaller players went to Butler because they were told by larger schools that they were too small to play the game. Hinkle proved that theory wrong time and again.

Considering the 1920s rules, one might think the game was a bit dull. But twelve thousand fans sat in awe when Tony Hinkle's team opened the big new fieldhouse and stopped Notre Dame on March 7, 1928. One Indianapolis sports reporter called it "a spectacular defensive battle . . . a thrilling contest from the first whistle. . . . The final issue was in doubt until the last three minutes when the Notre Dame defense cracked." The visitors led 11–9 in the first half, then scored only two more points the rest of the way. Butler's captain, Archie Chadd, put the Bulldogs ahead for the first time, only to have Notre Dame tie it. Late in the game, Harold Holz scored three field goals and a free throw to put the game away for Butler, 21–13.

The only thing that went wrong for Butler that first night was the collapse of some temporary bleachers just before the tipoff. Two hundred fifty people were thrown to the ground, including members of the Butler band. Thirteen spectators were injured, none seriously, but two were hospitalized.

Members of the team recall no reporters rushing down into the dressing room to talk to Hinkle or the players after that historic win, and the coach held no after-game session with the press. But Hinkle always maintained a casual relationship with the media, which then were primarily newspapers. He was accessible, except when he wanted to talk to his team at halftime. However, it should be noted that in the first years of the fieldhouse, members of the press had to work their way through the crowd to reach the locker room. They were located in an elevated press box which sits there abandoned still today. In those days, the floor ran east and west, following the configuration of the building. No one was happy with the arrangement. Members of the press said they were too inaccessible to information and most of the fans were viewing games from the two ends of the court. When the 1932–33 season opened, the floor was running north and south and the press was down on floor level.

Student reaction to what happened that opening night was an outpouring of pride and enthusiasm. Classes were dismissed the next day by President Robert Aley, though he refused to yield to student demands that the holiday be extended another day. Students made the most of it, holding a rally on campus and then moving downtown to stage a snake dance on Monument Circle. School yells and songs were spurred on by emotional speeches.

In all that show of emotion, Tony Hinkle was the exception. He wasn't an emotional speaker, but no doubt his subtle, underplayed style made a hit, if only by contrast. Tony was the student crowd's favorite. Just a few years out of college himself, he had led Butler to thirty-five basketball victories in forty-two games in his first two seasons as head coach. The young man whose life had started on Hoosier soil was getting the basketball world's attention in his home state. He had known some of the glory as a player at the widely respected University of Chicago; now he was beginning to experience it as a coach at a small, relatively unknown (at least nationally) university.

3 Hoosier Roots and the Move North

Paul Daniel (Tony) Hinkle's life began on a farm in north central Indiana, a few miles south of Logansport. Hinkle believed, though he was not certain, that his parents had first met when his mother, Winnie, was a student and his father, Edgar, was the teacher in a one-room schoolhouse in the area. The 125-acre farm was owned by Winnie's parents, Daniel and Sallie Ray. The Hinkles lived there because Edgar's income was meager. But Edgar was determined that the arrangement would be short-lived, for he wanted to rise to greater heights in his chosen field of education.

While Paul's maternal grandparents were landowners who symbolized stability, his paternal background was quite different. Edgar's mother, Harriett, died when he was six. His father, Lewis, remarried, but the son never felt accepted, according to Tony, and ran away. Edgar never lived with his father again. Tony said that his father grew up a "waif" in the Logansport area, living in barns wherever he could find an understanding family. But Edgar overcame that bleak childhood. He grew to be a highly motivated individual with high standards, standards he also demanded of his son. He became a father who was admired and respected.

Tony Hinkle's birth date was December 19, 1898, though he was always a little vague about just when his birth occurred. In 1970, when he retired, Butler thought it was exercising its mandatory age-seventy retirement regulation. Actually, Tony had turned seventy-one the previous December. Only years later did the university acknowledge that fact.

Hinkle often had fun with the subject. "I've always had trouble establishing the fact that I was born," he once told Tom Keating, the one-time *Indianapolis Star* columnist, "because out on the farm in those days, they registered the horses and the cows and the pigs, but the kids, they were a dime a dozen and I guess they didn't register me." On another occasion he said that a relative of his speculated that the doctor had filed the birth certificate at the Cass County courthouse in Logansport (though the farm where he was born was just over the line in Carroll County), and that it was lost along with a lot of other documents in the flood of 1912.

The early years of Edgar's career were a struggle, putting considerable demands on his wife and son. Ever determined to move ahead in teaching his specialty, mathematics, he obtained positions one school year at a time in various communities, always on the alert for a better-paying position the next year. Summers he took his family back to the farm and went back to school. During this time he earned a bachelor's degree at State Normal College (now Indiana State University in Terre Haute) and did graduate study at Indiana University, starting work toward a doctorate.

Teaching jobs took the family to various communities, including Goshen in Indiana, Winona in Minnesota, and Elgin in Illinois. Tony estimated that he was seven years old when his father got a job in the city that set the stage for young Hinkle's role in life. Edgar's first Chicago job was at Lakeview High School on the city's northside. Two years later he obtained a teaching position at the public school system's Chicago Normal College on the southside. The Hinkles moved to a nearby neighborhood, renting various apartments and homes in the area for the next few years. Tony was at Butler before his parents built and owned their own home. Edgar remained in the Chicago school system until he retired at age sixty-five.

One summer young Paul Daniel was out plowing a field with the help of two of Grandfather Ray's horses when he ran over a bee's nest. "Those bees came out and got me and the horses," Tony recalled some eighty years later, in 1989. "I stood it as long as I could, then I dumped the plow over and started running for home. I just got to the fence when my granddad met me. He gave me the damnedest licking I ever had in my life. That's when I found out a horse was more valuable than a kid."

Such educational summers at the farm were over by 1912, when the farm was sold after both grandparents died. Winnie and her sisters came into an inheritance. Along with Edgar's career advancements came more income, and that brought a better life for the Hinkle family. A daughter had been born just a few days before Paul's eleventh birthday. His baby sister was named Florence, and she and her brother remained close over the years despite the gap in their ages.

Florence Hinkle Lord looked back recently and said that Paul "caught hell for everything I did." When she broke a chair in one of their Chicago homes, Paul got the blame and accepted it without complaint. The only time he ever got stern with her was when he asked her why she didn't mind her mother. A retired teacher in Oak Lawn, a suburb west of Chicago, Florence felt that her brother's even temperament came from their mother. Both Paul and his mother were inclined to accept things and cope without trying to change them. In contrast, she saw herself as a fighter like their father. "We want something, we go out and fight for it," she said. "But they wouldn't."

Young Hinkle was extremely effective at coping, however. Once the Hinkles settled into Chicago's southside, Paul started getting involved in organized athletic endeavors at Hamilton Park, which offered physical education classes, probably at little or no cost. It was the first time he had remained in a neighborhood long enough to establish friendships.

Classes consisted of various calisthenic drills. Those who did them well were allowed to go outside and play basketball for fifteen minutes. They also played baseball, gathering and choosing up sides and having at it. A number of the boys were older, bigger, and stronger than Paul. Some of them made the games a full-time occupation and avoided school altogether. They were tough, rough kids and Edgar got worried about it. He called them bums and warned his son not to get involved with them. But young Hinkle coped. He followed his father's strict rules about school attendance and kept participating in the games at Hamilton Park. The encounters must have toughened him, for years later he said he didn't remember fearing injury in any sport he ever played.

It wasn't that Hinkle didn't know what it was like to suffer an injury. He was still in grade school when he broke his leg playing football. The game took place in a vacant lot. None of the participants had had any coaching and certainly no one possessed any equipment except the football. Hinkle was out of action for eight weeks and he remembered it years later as a "painful" experience.

Hinkle's football experience was further limited when the high school he was to attend dropped the sport before he ever enrolled. As he recalled it, some team members apparently were caught cheating on exams and the Chicago school system blew the whistle. So when Hinkle entered Calumet High School in the fall of 1912 he went out for the newly installed sport of soccer. He played defense, and in his senior year the team won the city high school championship.

The teenager was also successful in basketball and baseball at Calumet, though Hinkle told columnist Keating that the high school coach didn't really know much about basketball, "he'd just more or less keep us from fighting and pushing each other around. And that was about it." Hinkle also told Keating that he didn't play baseball on the high school team, that he learned the game playing at the park near his home. Nevertheless, the Calumet High School yearbook for 1916, Hinkle's graduation year, listed him as catcher. He was also pictured as a member of the baseball and golf teams.

Team results are not available at the high school, but Hinkle recalled that besides winning the city soccer championship, his basketball team went to the final game of the city basketball tournament in his senior year. He said he remembered that final game well because he played with an injured ankle, which his father treated with horse liniment. He laughed and said the liniment burned so badly he forgot about the injury.

It was a known fact at Butler that Hinkle wasn't an advocate of the art of running except as it was used for conditioning in preparation for other sports. Any good football prospect who tried to run cross country in the fall or any good baseball prospect who wanted to participate in spring track could expect an argument from Tony. A rare exception was the talented Tom Harding of the 1930s; he was allowed both to play baseball and to run track.

Few knew that Tony had attempted a little running once himself and had experienced embarrassment and annoyance over it. Eager to try all sports, he reported for track in high school one season. He was entered in the 660-yard dash at the Chicago city track meet. It was held at the city's old coliseum on a board track that had banked turns. The inexperienced Hinkle was one of some fifty runners in the event. He was in the outside lane and on the first turn was crowded over to the edge and over the bank. There is no evidence that he ever competed in any track event again.

The busy young athlete's parents were extremely important to him during this phase of his life. They were a close family, spending a lot of time together. Hinkle said his father was always willing to help him with his studies whenever he had a problem and his mother was always there fixing the meals and making sure Paul had all the comforts of home.

In Hinkle's junior year his father started taking him to football and basketball games at the nearby University of Chicago. One day Edgar asked Paul if he would like to play at that prestigious university. Paul thought it was an exciting idea. But something else happened first. Lake Forest College, located north of Chicago on the Lake Michigan shore, offered him an athletic scholarship. Young Hinkle was eager to accept. Edgar wasn't. He considered Paul's initial response a commitment, and that's how Paul Hinkle ended up enrolling at Chicago.

4 Undergraduate Days

Stories about Tony Hinkle's cautious attitude toward spending his or Butler's money are legion. If he could avoid spending it, he did.

Hinkle's long-time assistant coach, Bob Dietz, recalled a trip to New York when he was playing basketball for Hinkle. It was probably during the 1939–40 season when Butler played in Madison Square Garden against powerful Long Island University and a legendary coach, Clair Bee. Coach Hinkle complimented the players on their effort—they lost in front of a large partisan crowd by only two points—and said he would give them some money so they could "go out on the town." He handed them each fifty cents.

The coach's thrift was understandable. The father he admired had always been that way, and in fact Edgar's frugal attitude figured into his decision that his son should go to the University of Chicago. The Hinkles lived four miles from the campus, and money could be saved if Paul lived at home. Even a scholarship at Lake Forest couldn't beat that, since Paul would almost certainly have to live near the Lake Forest campus.

But frugality wasn't the whole story. Edgar knew that his son would get a proper education at Chicago and that he would be nearby if Paul had any academic problems. Hinkle's dad also realized that his son would be heavily involved in athletics, and he greatly admired the two men who would be coaching and working with Paul: the athletic director and football coach, Amos Alonzo Stagg, and the basketball and baseball coach, Harlan (Pat) Page.

Stagg had played four years of football at Yale as an end. He was not a big man. He was described as a stocky five feet ten. His Yale team had lost only one game in four seasons, and Stagg had been named to the first all-American football team in 1888. He had come to Chicago in 1892 to set up the university's athletic program. He originally thought he was going to be a minister, and he held to a strict moral code that he also demanded of his athletes. Hinkle never forgot the aura of the man. "We admired him very much, but we always were scared of him too," Hinkle said in 1989. "He was a funny guy. He didn't let you get too close to him and he had a way of keeping you off balance. We had great big respect for him. If he was walkin' down one side of the street and we were on the same side as he and we'd see him coming, we'd go across the street, to miss him."

A history of the Big Ten compiled by Kenneth (Tug) Wilson and Jerry Brondfield credited Stagg with pioneering a long list of football basics, including the T formation, the quick kick, the man-in-motion, the fake handoff, the flanker, crossblocking, and the double-delayed pass. Although historians agree that Stagg could have been a successful major league pitcher, the opportunity to develop a collegiate athletic program was far more to his liking.

Students of Tony Hinkle find some parallels between Stagg and the youth who was enrolling at Chicago in the fall of 1916. Stagg was never known to recruit an athlete (Hinkle didn't relish it), and he remained at his university forty years until he was forced to retire at the age of seventy (the same rule that ended Hinkle's coaching career at Butler). Unlike Hinkle, however, Stagg affiliated with another school and coached football for fourteen more years. That was at College (now University) of the Pacific. He then accepted assistant football coaching jobs that he filled until he was ninety-three. He died at age 102.

Pat Page was an apt student of Stagg's and had been a star athlete at Chicago just a few years before Hinkle enrolled. Parallels also appear between Page and Hinkle. Page lettered in football, basketball, and baseball (Hinkle did the same), and both earned nine letter awards, three in each of the sports mentioned. (The only other University of Chicago athlete who ever achieved that distinction was Herbert Orrin [Fritz] Crisler, a teammate of Hinkle's. Crisler became a highly successful football coach and athletic director at the University of Michigan.) Both Page and Hinkle figured prominently in achieving Big Ten basketball championships during their playing days. Both ended up in the Naismith Basketball Hall of Fame, as did Stagg.

Hinkle recalled that Page was a contrast to Stagg, whom the players called "the old man." He described Page as "a lot of fun," though a hard taskmaster. Players had a closer relationship with Page, who of course was a lot nearer their age, having graduated in 1910.

When young Paul enrolled at the University of Chicago, he was entering a school that had won five of the first twenty season championships in football in the Western Conference, or Big Ten. Inexperienced in this sport, Hinkle got a year of preparation on the freshman squad, coached by Page. He weighed 155 pounds when he reported for his initial practice, and when asked what position he played, he said, "Anywhere." Page assigned him to a spot on the line, as guard. The freshmen played no schedule of their own. Their primary job was to scrimmage against the varsity. Hinkle recalled that the first day, "naturally I didn't know too much about it so I just tried to get that guy who had the ball; that's about all I knew . . . and I know I got the hell kicked out of me."

Hinkle learned his lessons well, and before that first season was over he was playing end. He proved to Page and others that he could catch a ball and run. That assignment didn't exactly put Hinkle in the spotlight his first year on the varsity, though. Stagg believed in passing only on third down when long yardage was needed for a first down. (That was forty years ahead of "three yards and a cloud of dust" advocates Woody Hayes and Bo Schembechler.)

Stagg also was a proponent of physical conditioning. A series of twenty-yard wind sprints always came at the end of practice, usually after dark. Hinkle told Keating that one time when he was "loping a little bit like the rest of them," Stagg picked him out to discipline. " 'Hinkle! Stay after this is over and run a hundred twenty-yard wind sprints!' And by god, he stayed there and saw that I ran one hundred twenty-yard wind sprints. He was that kind of guy."

Earning a letter in football playing for Stagg as a sophomore was not easy. The eleven starters played most of the game, offensively and defensively. Injury was the main cause for a player's removal, and the rules prevented any removed player from reentering. But Hinkle did earn his letter in 1917 on a team that had a so-so record of three wins, two losses, and one tie at a time when many young men began going into military service in World War I.

Basketball was a far more familiar sport to Hinkle than football, and yet the 1917 University of Chicago yearbook, *Cap and Gown*, did not list him among the top varsity prospects in its summary of the freshman season. A year later that changed. The student publication was impressed with Hinkle's first season on the varsity, when the team posted six wins and six losses: "Hinkle was an ideal guard, clever with his pivots and a quick thinker. His basket shooting at long range won games singlehanded."

In baseball, Hinkle moved rapidly into prominence. He was captain of the freshman team, and in his sophomore year he was pitching and playing left field on a varsity that won two-thirds of its games. He was described as fast in the outfield and a good base runner. The yearbook also pointed out that Hinkle won "a good number of games" as a pitcher. By his junior year he had been moved to shortstop when he wasn't pitching and would bat cleanup.

Baseball almost ended Hinkle's athletic career at the university. As many young men did in those days, he played semiprofessional baseball on the side. Such games were played in the public parks on the southside of Chicago, and he could pick up fifteen to twenty dollars a game. No one played under his real name. One year Hinkle was "Rawls," another year he was "Black." It was against the rules, and Stagg got wind of it. He called Hinkle into his office and threatened to rule him ineligible. Quite out of character, the kid from Logansport stood up to "the old man" and said he had no proof. The head of the Chicago park system came to Hinkle's defense, and that apparently saved him. Stagg never mentioned it again.

Hinkle tangled with Stagg on one other occasion. The coach wanted him to report for spring football practice, which conflicted with baseball, and told him that if he didn't opt for football, he wouldn't play anymore. Again Hinkle held his ground, and nothing more was said.

Hinkle recalled that he picked up his specialty, the spitball pitch, during his summer days as a teenager playing with the "bums" in Hamilton Park. He said he got a little advice here and there and eventually was able to control the pitch. He used slippery elm, which he bought at a drugstore for five cents for a year's supply. The idea was to chew it, then wet one's hands and massage the baseball. It was perfectly legal until 1921, when the spitball was outlawed for anyone going into professional baseball. The decision convinced Hinkle that his future looked brighter in coaching, though he kept playing.

It was during his second year at the university that Paul Daniel Hinkle acquired the nickname Tony. According to Hinkle, Coach Page coined it during a road trip when Hinkle came out of a restaurant carrying an extra serving of spaghetti and meatballs. The nickname became a permanent part of Hinkle's life, but the

Hinkle family never really accepted it. His parents and his sisters (his second sister, Lois, was born after Hinkle joined the Butler athletic staff) always referred to him as Paul.

Life at the university was busy for young Hinkle. Freshmen were subjected to hazing by the student body, and daily sessions were held in which, Hinkle told Keating, the younger students were required to perform such antics as "singing in front of the students, and gettin' up in a tree and chirping like a bird and all kinds of stunts of that nature." When he pledged a fraternity, he was unaware of the demands it would place on his time. He was due to be initiated on the same day he was scheduled to play in his church basketball team's city championship game. Somehow he managed to show up for both activities.

Hinkle's daily athletic practice sessions were practically year round, since once one sport ended another began. His choice of classes and his studying for them were carefully monitored by his father. Florence recalled that her brother was always home all day Sunday studying and that he was very serious about it. Eventually he became interested in oil geology and decided on that for his major. Edgar, described by Tony as "the smart one in the family," heartily agreed, convinced there was a bright future in that field of endeavor.

Fortunately for the young student-athlete, his father covered most of his expenses, wanting him to put all his effort into school demands. His school costs seem minuscule today. The school year consisted of three quarters, and tuition was forty dollars a quarter. Tony received twenty-five cents a day from his father. Ten cents went for his round-trip streetcar fare. That left fifteen cents for his lunch and made it necessary for him to go home if he wanted dinner. Even for a distinguished three-sport athlete the university provided no financial help.

Social life was minimal for Hinkle. Though he found some of the coeds attractive, he didn't date because he didn't have the time, it wasn't important, and he didn't have an automobile.

In the fall of 1918 the school felt the impact of the war. The entire University of Chicago football team voted to join the Student Army Training Corps (SATC), convinced it was a better move than allowing themselves to be drafted. What they didn't count on was the resulting orders that eleven of them should report for active-duty immediately. Hinkle never overcame his suspicions about the timing of the orders. The head of the SATC at Chicago was a Purdue graduate, and the orders came just a few days before Chicago was to play Purdue, a school the Maroons had dominated in football. Needless to say, Chicago lost that game and all the others that season.

Tony was one of the eleven who was sent to Camp MacArthur at Waco, Texas, in September to begin officer training. His service included playing football for the military base with practically no protective equipment. Fellow student Fritz Crisler, who had also joined the active duty group, dislocated his shoulder during a game. Tony said that Crisler was hauled away in an ambulance pulled by two horses. It was a bumpy ride, and during one of the bumps his shoulder went back in place.

A few weeks later the war ended and the men were free to return to civilian life if they so wished. Hinkle and Crisler were back at the University of Chicago in late December in time for the basketball season. Hinkle had been named captain, an honor he retained for his final two seasons. Crisler was about as inexperienced in basketball as Hinkle had been in football, and he was a year behind Hinkle in school. Nevertheless, he became a back guard, a primarily defensive position, and Hinkle was at the other guard position, bringing the ball down the court and setting up the offense. Hinkle was praised for his defensive as well as his offensive work on that team, which went undefeated until the last two games, only to lose both. Hinkle was named to the all-conference team, and the yearbook called him one of the greatest guards in the school's history.

Hinkle's last basketball season at Chicago, 1919–20, was even brighter. With all but one regular back in action, the team won the Big Ten championship. The yearbook was ecstatic: "Captain

Paul Hinkle is undoubtedly one of the greatest guards who ever played for Chicago or any other conference team. . . . 'Tony' plays a remarkable floor game, made possible by his dribbling and pivoting. Although he scored enough points to lead the regular conference guards this season, Hinkle was always back on defense in time to cover the best of forwards."

A few months before Hinkle's last basketball season opened, the Chicago baseball team traveled across the Pacific for a five-week tour of Japan. They played fourteen games with a half-dozen university baseball teams before enthusiastic crowds. Japan had taken to the game with gusto. The trip, the third for the university, was declared a success. The team won eight of its fourteen games and two were declared ties.

During the trip the Japanese insisted on holding a demonstration basketball game. The Champions of Tokyo were defeated by the Chicago group, 70–0. A second game was played in Osaka, and since the Chicago team had left their shoes in Tokyo, the Japanese had special shoes made for their visitors, including Hinkle and Crisler. The Maroons won that one also, 40–0. Years later Hinkle recalled, "They were kinda little and I guess we didn't show much mercy."

Hinkle had two seasons of football eligibility left when he returned from army service in late 1918. He also needed more time to complete his course work, since army service and the Japan trip had deprived him of two of the twelve quarters normally needed to complete work for graduation. So it was back to toiling for "the old man" in the fall of 1919 on Stagg's first post–World War I team.

Hinkle was eager, and far more knowledgeable now about Stagg's style. He was unlikely to repeat the kind of gaffe he made during his sophomore year when Stagg had told to warm up in preparation for entering the game. Hinkle ran up and down the sidelines over and over and over. Finally deciding that Stagg had forgotten about him, he sat down. As Hinkle told Keating, "About the second I sat down, he says, 'Hinkle, I thought I told you to warm up? Touche, get in there.' Touche was my substitute; and he put him in and kept me out." Although Stagg was quick to confront and criticize his players, Hinkle never heard him swear. About the worst thing he called anyone was a "jackass," although in extremity one might be called a "double jackass."

The 1919 Chicago team, with Hinkle and Crisler the ends, produced five wins—but also two losses, both to Big Ten teams. One of them was to Iowa. The Hawkeyes were on the Maroon twenty-yard line when Hinkle was put in to stop an anticipated pass. As he entered he called out, "Come on, boys." A rule in effect at the time stated that a player entering the game could talk to no one. So Chicago was penalized fifteen yards, and that put Iowa on the five-yard line. The rule, which had been formed to prevent the sending of instructions from the sidelines, a common practice today, was rescinded shortly afterward.

In Hinkle's last season as an athlete at Chicago the football team was picked for a second-division finish in the Big Ten. After a fast start, the squad faltered and lost its last four Big Ten games. Hinkle was called the best pass catcher on the team even though he was hampered by injuries.

Hinkle's career at Chicago was over—or was it? Pat Page had resigned the previous spring to tackle the athletic program at Butler. Stagg appointed himself acting basketball coach and asked Hinkle to be his assistant as Hinkle continued taking courses to qualify for graduation. Early in 1921 Page sent for Hinkle to join him at Butler. Major league baseball manager John McGraw also asked Hinkle to report to the New York Giants, but the spitball ruling ended that option. Stagg was startled and seemingly offended when Hinkle informed him of his decision to go to Butler, but Stagg had not indicated that he wanted Hinkle to stay at Chicago. If he had, Hinkle might never have gone to Butler. But go he did, and the stage was set for the creation of a Butler legend.

5 Launching of a Legend

Tony Hinkle couldn't have arrived at Butler at a better time. A whole new attitude toward athletics was developing, and Hinkle had been selected to become a part of it. His old basketball coach at the University of Chicago had decided Hinkle was the man he wanted to be his overall assistant in carrying out the school's new, more aggressive program.

For the first time in the school's history, an athletic department had been established with full-time paid personnel. In the past, dedicated alumni who had lettered at the school had coached on a part-time basis for little or no compensation. The last of these volunteers in football, the primary sport, was Joe Mullane, who fully supported a proposal, framed by a prominent group of alumni, to put the school on a more competitive basis. The proposal came during a winless, one-touchdown season. In fact, the Bulldogs had managed only two wins over the two preceding seasons. In basketball, their meager five-game schedule in 1918–19 produced one win.

Actually, Butler had a rather impressive history, not only in basketball but also in football, in terms of longevity. Its first football team was formed in 1885, and it swept a three-game schedule in 1887, the first year for which scores are available. One of its victims was Purdue, by a score of 45–5. The school also had a baseball team that school year that went 0–2.

For five school years beginning in 1899, Walter Kelly had served as athletic director, and he set a precedent that was picked up by Hinkle: Kelly coached all sports teams. He also became a successful Irvington physician and practiced for many years. Perhaps in the early days he had few patients.

After Kelly left the campus, matters somehow got out of hand. Early in 1906 the school administration announced it was suspending all intercollegiate sports competition. The only exceptions were instances where the basketball team already had contract commitments. The action was taken after the school held an internal investigation. According to the *Butler Collegian*, this followed accusations by the press and the Indiana Intercollegiate Athletic Association that some football team members at Butler were being paid or were receiving other inducements. Within a few months the accusers apparently were satisfied that proper action had been taken. Butler resumed competition in time for the 1906 seasons with new coaches in both football and basketball.

Just prior to World War I, the university began to inch its way toward establishing a stronger athletic philosophy. That attitude was encouraged considerably by the presence on campus of George Cullen Thomas. Cully, as he was affectionately known, was the campus hero at Butler for four years. While earning a degree in chemistry, he starred in five sports (football, basketball, baseball, tennis, track), and he is the only man in the history of Butler to earn eighteen varsity letters.

Cully became athletic director (the unconfirmed salary was one thousand dollars annually) and coached football, basketball, and baseball. But with little or no professional assistance even Butler's "finest" couldn't quite keep up with the competition. Competing schools were beginning to add to their coaching staffs and strengthen their budgets. Thomas left after the 1918 football season to pursue a successful career with General Mills, eventually becoming chairman of the board.

When Cully left, the faculty took over the running of the athletic program. In effect the program was removed from mainstream competition and absorbed by academia. The school was at a turning point, and the alumni, many of whom lived in Irvington, convinced the university that athletics had more pluses than minuses for the future of the institution. Enter Pat Page.

Schooled in Stagg's successful Chicago tradition, Page brought energy and aggressiveness to Butler athletics. He was easy to like, and he could induce response. He inherited virtually the same football team in 1920 that had failed to win a game the previous season. That 1919 team lost two lettermen. Page won seven of eight games, and the team outscored its opponents 251–51.

Basketball had run second to football at Butler. Page changed that. In 1919, after the school converted the vacated army structure to a basketball facility, Page had additional bleachers installed so that most of the six hundred students could see the home games.

Page's first basketball team was a hit. Captained by Rowland Jones, who later became long-time coach and athletic director at Washington High School in Indianapolis, the team won sixteen of nineteen games, including one over Page's alma mater.

Tony Hinkle thus arrived at Butler when enthusiasm was at a new high among both students and alumni, who were enjoying a new era of athletic achievement. Hinkle accepted Page's offer in February 1921 to be assistant athletic director and help him in coaching. Page immediately showed the extent of the confidence he had in Tony by letting him take over the baseball program.

Tony coached the baseball team in the spring of 1921 and most of the baseball teams until his retirement. His third Butler nine became the first of the school's teams to compete on the new campus at Fairview Park. Relocation was four years away when a diamond was laid out on what is now the grassy mall between Jordan Hall and the library. Home plate was at the north end, now identified by a commemorative marker. Players came to bat looking southward. Game day, May 17, 1924, was designated "Fairview Day," and blue and white pennants were displayed, designating locations of buildings and boulevards yet to come. The president of the Butler Board of Trustees, Hilton U. Brown, threw out the first ball to launch the game at 2:30 P.M. Hinkle had arranged to have his old alma mater provide the competition, and it obliged even to the extent of losing. With an estimated two thousand fans there to watch, the University of Chicago lost when the Blue Sox came up with two big innings. The score was 8–6.

Page personally handled football, basketball, track, cross country, and tennis his first school year at Butler, 1920–21. After that, he concentrated on football and basketball with Hinkle at his side.

Although the new assistant wasn't much older than many of the players, he had no problem earning their respect. Dave Konold, a 1926 graduate, remembered Hinkle's 1920s style vividly: "He was tough but he wasn't a shouter and one who would rake you over the coals all the time. He would explain your faults and tell you how to correct them instead of bawling you out. He was a gentle sort of coach. You knew he knew what he was talking about; there wasn't any question about that." And Bob Nipper, a member of the same class as Konold, recalled how Hinkle impressed him in his role as assistant: "He'd get after you if he didn't think your feet were moving fast enough. I've never seen a fellow create quick feet. He could do it. He could speed you up without any effort and the first thing you know you're flitting right and left."

Hinkle also scouted for Page. Once Page had studied Hinkle's analysis of an upcoming opponent he would have his young assistant scrimmage, demonstrating the style of key players. Hinkle earned respect with those performances. Konold recalled that particularly in football Hinkle was "a rough one" and "strong physically."

Evidence indicates that Tony went to Butler at a salary of fifty dollars a week. But he seldom passed up a chance to earn extra money as long as it didn't interfere with Butler assignments. He played professional basketball with a number of midwestern squads, an activity that was permitted by universities at the time. Hinkle said he averaged seventy-five dollars a game, which was incentive enough to participate as much as possible. His most frequent appearances were with the Indianapolis Omars and teams based in Fort Wayne and Paxton, Illinois. In fact, Hinkle got his first look at the Butler campus when he was in Indianapolis to play for the Fort Wayne Knights of Columbus team.

Periodically teams would contact him for a specific game when they wanted to match his skills against a player about whom they were particularly concerned. Tony would catch an interurban or a train to get to an out-of-town game and get back in time to handle his Butler workload.

Hinkle also took officiating assignments. One night in Martinsville he made a controversial call against the home team. The player's name was John Wooden. As Hinkle told the story in 1989, "He was a great dribbler. He'd dribble and dribble and dribble around people. So he dribbled and hit a guy and I called a charging foul. I thought I was going to get thrown out of town, calling a foul on Wooden." Wooden was reminded of that incident in an interview in 1990. He said he didn't remember the night in question but added: "Tony Hinkle at that age was a great athlete in his own right at the University of Chicago. He wasn't fearful of anything. He's just stretchin' it a little bit."

The young athlete's first summer in Indianapolis was spent in part with the Indianapolis Indians baseball club. In an interview with John Bansch of the *Indianapolis Star* in 1970, Hinkle said he was signed to pitch for the club but his Indians career was cut short when Cincinnati sent a player to the American

Association club. Hinkle said he was cut by the Indians and went to Spartanburg. That team clinched a pennant early and he was reassigned to LaGrange, Georgia, a team that also won a pennant. Once again he was released to another team, and that convinced him his professional baseball career was over.

The next summer Tony went back to Chicago to complete the one course he still needed to qualify him for his bachelor's degree. He divided his time by working at Chicago's Jackson Park and playing golf.

During at least two more summers, Hinkle lived at his parents' home in Chicago, held summer jobs, and played more baseball. The baseball usually was linked to the job. That was the case one summer when he held the title chief electrician at a steel company in Gary and "didn't know a damn thing" about what he was supposed to be doing. But such summers were numbered as he became more and more immersed in his life at Butler.

The early 1920s were learning years for Tony. He wasn't learning about a particular sport. He'd had that course. He was observing how a successful coach operated. Page was very much in charge, and Hinkle's role was to carry out assignments. That was no problem, and the program continued to prosper. Page was recruiting high school stars from around the state through Hinkle and the cooperation of alumni, particularly those affiliated with fraternities. It was acceptable at the time for alumni to provide financial help to needy athletes.

Hinkle's first year as assistant in football, 1921, was the year Haldane Griggs enrolled. A graduate of nearby Arsenal Technical High School, he became a multi-sports star. His specialties were the place kick in football and jumping in basketball, so critical in the center jump era. When he was a sophomore Griggs's kicking ability was the element in a win over the University of Illinois at Champaign. It was the first nonconference loss for the Illini in twenty years. Two weeks later twelve thousand persons jammed Butler's Irwin Field to see Griggs score all the points in a close win over big rival Wabash. For years Griggs held the school's record for the longest football field goal scored, fifty-two yards. In Griggs's junior year in basketball, the team won the Amateur Athletic Union national championship in a tournament at Kansas City.

Page's basketball teams at Butler produced records such as the school had never seen before, with ninety-four victories and twenty-nine defeats. Five of the six seasons he coached produced heavy winners. Then suddenly the Pat Page era ended abruptly. Page resigned just before the last basketball game in 1926. There was a student protest, but the administration assured the student body that Page had not been forced out. Less than a month later, he became head football coach at Indiana University.

6 Coping, Courting, and Coaching

Many years later one can still find Butler alumni who are convinced that Page was forced to resign his athletic posts at Butler. He had brought the school into the mainstream of collegiate athletics as it prepared to move to a new campus and impressive new athletic facilities. The school administration expressed shock and dismay at the resignation. However, one official indicated that Page had talked with him previously about leaving, possibly at the end of the school year.

Ironically, success may have contributed to Page's departure. His teams became popular with more and more students, alumni, and fans throughout the area. They willingly purchased tickets, and probably for the first time in the history of the school, athletics became a revenue producer. Income was further enhanced because Page scheduled bonus games on road trips for basketball. Unheard of today and of course beyond the rules now, these games were frequently with teams that were professional. Bob Nipper, who played four years of basketball and football for Page (before the school barred freshmen from varsity competition) estimated that the take for Page was anywhere from seven hundred to eight hundred dollars a game. Nipper also said the money was deposited in an Irvington bank for athletic purposes. As the fund grew, insiders say, the Butler administration got more and more concerned, feeling that the university, not Page, should be deciding how the money was used. The theory goes that Page was going to have to relinquish control of the fund, and that led to his displeasure and departure.

Within a month, Tony was named to assume Page's primary assignments as acting athletic director and head football and basketball coach. It seemed appropriate. Hinkle had certainly contributed to Page's success as his chief assistant over the preceding five years. It wasn't going to be easy, however, especially in football. Eleven men on Page's last team had graduated, including key members of the squad.

Page left without taking assistant Otto Strohmeier, another acquisition from the University of Chicago. But he did take Hugh (Wally) Middlesworth, who had starred for him in both football and basketball. Hinkle named Nipper, who was just graduating, to serve as freshman coach.

Hinkle's first football team, in 1926, started with one-sided wins at Irwin Field over Earlham and Hanover, then lost six of the next seven games. The most embarrassing loss was at the University of Minnesota, where the Bulldogs were treated mercilessly, 81–0.

Bill Bugg was one of the many sophomores on that team. He was a starter who played tackle on offense and linebacker on defense. Bugg recalled that Hinkle never scolded the team, confining his comments to those of a constructive nature. The morale on the team was excellent, and Tony was well-liked and respected. In Bugg's opinion, Hinkle felt he was getting the best out of what he had.

One of the few seniors on the team was Frank Teague, who became an Indianapolis physician. Having played for both Page and Hinkle, Teague felt that Tony was far more receptive than Page to one-on-one conversation if a player initiated it and would also offer advice about non-football concerns if asked.

Two incidents probably reveal what was going on inside Hinkle that season. The team finale was at the University of Dayton. Play was less than inspired, and the Bulldogs trailed at halftime. In the locker room, with the entire squad present, Hinkle and his assistant, Strohmeier, got into a shouting match, presumably over what should be done about Butler's dilemma. It ended in a fist fight, and one witness said the young head coach came in second. Strohmeier left shortly afterward for a return trip to Chicago. The other incident came at the season-ending awards ceremony: Hinkle gave major awards only to seniors. Most of the others got secondary awards, with an assurance that they would get major awards the next year if they came back and made good.

But Hinkle did not get to make the final decisions that next year. A former star at the University of Illinois, George (Potsy) Clark, was named to take over from Hinkle as football coach and to assume the job of athletic director.

When Tony tackled his head basketball assignment that first year, he had far better results than in football. Who would have guessed that when Hinkle traveled to Danville, Indiana, on Saturday, December 11, 1926, such a lengthy and memorable basketball scenario was starting? Tony's first opponent was Central Normal (a school that no longer exists), and the start was nothing remarkable, a 28–24 victory. There would be sixteen more that season. Among the victims: University of Chicago (twice), Marquette (twice), Michigan State (twice), Iowa, and Illinois. The season record was seventeen wins, four losses.

Captain of that team was Bob Wakefield, who grew up and remained in Ben Davis, at the western edge of Indianapolis. Wakefield had played basketball for Tony as a freshman in 1923–24, the first year Butler had freshman teams, so he knew what to expect of the new head coach. He said that Page, for whom he played his sophomore and junior years, never had a set plan on offense, only on defense. Hinkle changed that, and the players responded. Something else changed. Hinkle never dressed a player down in front of the team. Serious matters were always discussed in private. Wakefield was a top scorer on Tony's first basketball team, with 146 points as a forward. The men awarded letters on Hinkle's first basketball squad besides Wakefield were Bill Bugg, Clarence Christopher, Archie Chadd (later a highly successful Indiana high school coach), Dana Chandler, Walter Floyd, Alan Fromuth, Harold Holz, and Frank White.

It was a happy time for Tony. His baseball team broke even that season, but overall he had winners four out of seven seasons, with many of the basketball players participating. Then in mid- July the Clark decision was revealed. Tony had a new boss.

Clark went to Butler with eleven years of coaching experience. He had headed programs at the University of Kansas and Michigan State (which didn't join the Big Ten until 1950). At the time of his appointment to the Butler job he was assistant head football coach at Minnesota.

It was a definite setback for Hinkle. Not only was he removed as athletic director and football coach, but Clark moved him out as baseball coach, too. Potsy took that job his first season, then handed it to Wee Willie McGill the next. But Tony was typically Tony. As his sister Florence observed, he didn't show his feelings to outsiders. He just kept plugging away at the task at hand.

With Archie Chadd as captain, Tony's second basketball team, in 1927–28, won nineteen of twenty-two games and the Indiana Collegiate Conference title the second straight year. The biggest game of that season came at the end against Notre Dame in the new fieldhouse.

There was still greater joy for Hinkle that year. Sometime, probably in 1927, he went alone to a popular cafeteria in Irvington for his evening meal and was smitten by the sight of a beautiful young woman who was dining at the same place that evening with her mother. No one can resurrect just what transpired the next few moments but the scene was set for a courtship. Jane Murdock was about twenty and Tony was approaching twenty-eight. Jane followed sports and probably was aware of Hinkle's identity. She worked at the Fletcher National Bank, probably at the branch in the heart of Irvington. A native of Lafayette, Jane attended Indiana University before going to Indianapolis to complete a secretarial course at Central Business College. She has been described as a gregarious, fun-loving person who was just right as a mate for a serious-minded athlete who was establishing himself as a successful coach.

She also was adept at getting her way. Hinkle's strategy on the basketball court and football field was no match for Jane's clever maneuvering to talk Tony into taking her to a certain spot for dinner. But Tony was a willing victim. There also is a theory that the school administration encouraged the courtship and was quite happy over the thought that the single, handsome all-American from Chicago might become a husband. The only other woman anyone remembered Tony dating was Eleanor Twitchell, whom he apparently met in Chicago. Eleanor became Mrs. Lou Gehrig.

Tony and Jane were married on the last day of June in 1928 at eleven o'clock in the morning at the Marott Hotel in Indianapolis. It was a private event; only a few persons were present. Tony's parents and two sisters were there, and presumably the groom's father was best man. One story has Tony so nervous about the event that he spent much of his wedding night walking around the block outside.

After a short honeymoon, Jane and Tony settled down in an apartment on North Meridian Street near the campus. Not long after their marriage, Jane learned that she would have to share her husband's life with athletics, which severely competed for his time and attention. That meant some lonely and unhappy times, which were difficult to accept. But she also was married to a man who had strong feelings about family ties. Jane never missed a home football or basketball game. When she suggested going on road trips, however, she quickly learned that her husband didn't approve of her going.

Hinkle continued to keep in close touch with his parents during those early years at Butler. They depended on him to keep them informed about how his teams were doing, since Chicago newspapers provided little information on Butler and radio sports coverage then was minimal. On those occasions when Butler came to play the University of Chicago, the family turned out. Their visits to Indianapolis were limited to summertime because of Edgar's busy schedule in the Chicago school system.

The 1928–29 basketball season was Hinkle's best yet. The team went 17–2 and was declared national collegiate champion by the Veterans Athletic Association of Philadelphia. While even Butler's yearbook, the *Drift*, admitted that it was almost impossible to determine a national champion, there were some impressive wins that season. Among the victims were defending Big Ten co-champions Purdue and Illinois and the national champions of the previous season, Pittsburgh. Pitt had won twenty-seven straight games when it succumbed. Other wins came over the Southern Conference champion, North Carolina, and Missouri, considered strongest in the Missouri Valley Conference that season.

The first encounter of the season with Notre Dame took place at the Butler Fieldhouse on Friday night, February 15. Butler had lost only one game, while the visitors had four losses. Most of the ten thousand persons on hand expected a Bulldog win. It didn't happen. The hosts had an off night and lost 24–21. Three weeks later at South Bend, Butler won 35–16. That win probably was the deciding factor in getting the national championship.

Hinkle's roster for the Notre Dame game was what would become a typical Hinkle collection of homegrown talent. The souvenir program for that game listed ten players, four from the immediate Indianapolis area, four from other places in central Indiana, one from Terre Haute, and one from Fort Wayne. Only four were seniors. Half of the team would go into coaching (Wilbur Allen, William Bugg, Jake Caskey, and Cleon Reynolds) and one, Oral Hildebrand, would go on to pitch for ten years in the American League, including a World Series start with the champion Yankees in 1940, his final year. Others on that team were captain Frank White, Dana Chandler, Marshall Christopher, Alan Fromuth, and Maurice Hosier. When Tony was honored at his retirement in 1970, all but Hosier were still living. Eight of the nine were present at the fieldhouse that night.

Bugg felt that Hinkle's attitude and his emphasis on fundamentals played a definite part in the success of the 1928–29 team and the two that preceded it. "Tony was good on fundamentals from the beginning," Bugg said in 1989. "Sometimes he would go out on the floor and spend twenty-five minutes participating in one drill." And when it came to handling a moody player, Bugg made this observation: "Hildebrand was an excellent ball player but he was like a little boy. If something went bad out on the floor not to his liking, he just took off and went up into the bleachers and sat down [during practice]. Somebody said something about it to Tony and Tony said, 'Just leave him alone. He'll change his mind. He'll be back down. He's just a kid. He'll get over it.' That's exactly what happened. Tony just didn't make a scene of it."

Bugg, who also played on the football team, said there was definite resentment among team members when Clark moved into the football program in 1927 and Tony was demoted. Most of the basketball team played football then and many played baseball. Page and Hinkle had set a pattern, drawing on their own experiences as participants in more than one sport. They had looked for people who were willing to do that on the basis that all-round athletes were probably better athletes. That philosophy continued through the 1930s and to a lesser degree until 1970.

Clark performed no miracles his first football season. The team went 4–3–1 and received sound whippings from Illinois and Michigan State. But things got better as more and more players from upper Minnesota began enrolling. The next two seasons Clark's teams won ten of sixteen games, and by 1929 all but two of the opponents were schools from out of state with what were considered at the time to be strong football programs.

Clark was in charge when Butler played its first game in the new Butler Bowl. Original plans called for a stadium seating seventy-five thousand. The first phase of the construction was about half that, however, and it never got any larger. Seating capacity was further reduced (by approximately sixteen thousand) when the Starlight Musicals Theatron was constructed at the south end of the Bowl in 1955.

Surprisingly, only seven thousand attended Butler's first game in the Bowl on October 13, 1928. The schedule called for only minor opposition that day, and maybe that was a factor. Franklin College was the victim. It had provided formidable competition in basketball, but football was a different story that year. Butler scored at will and won 55–0. Four weeks later the dedication game attracted twice as many spectators when the University of Illinois was the opponent. The Illini prevailed 14–0 on a muddy field. Clark won six of eight that year and then went 4–4 in 1929, a season that ended with a Thanksgiving Day win over Loyola of New Orleans in the Bowl.

It had been four years since Pat Page's departure and the shock waves that accompanied it. Then, early in 1930, the North Central Association of Colleges and Universities announced it was suspending Butler from its accredited list. Its primary reason was that Butler was overemphasizing athletics.

7 Suspension, Reinstatement, and Promotion

Tony Hinkle was in no way implicated in the North Central suspension, but there is still talk today by athletes and staff who were at Butler at the time about the way Potsy Clark operated. The talk is that "some people downtown" funneled funds unofficially to the campus and that the money was distributed to football players recruited by Clark—many of them "muscular heavyweights" from Ohio, upper Minnesota, and Michigan. The suspension order, however, never mentioned improper subsidization of Butler athletes. It zeroed in on the athletic program generally.

The North Central Association challenged the expenditure of $750,000 for a fieldhouse, gymnasium, and football field for such a small university. The association called Clark's salary of ten thousand dollars a year exorbitant and accused the school of overextending itself to the detriment of its endowment, which the association considered too small; it also didn't like the way the money was being raised. In addition, the association called the library inadequate and the faculty-student ratio too high.

Officially, athletic funds were being handled by a separate corporation of prominent Indianapolis businessmen (some of them Butler alumni) who were selling stock for the cause. The *Drift* described it as an "incorporated body of forty-one Indianapolis businessmen and financiers, alumni and friends of the University" and stated that in "cooperating with the university Board of Directors and other executives, this corporation has control of Butler's athletics."

Butler's response to the criticism was that the fieldhouse was not intended to be used exclusively by Butler. The administration pointed out that the building was to be made available to the community and that the Indiana High School Athletic Association had agreed to use it for the next fifteen years for the annual state high school basketball tournament if its seating space was increased. That is why the school raised the capacity to fifteen thousand.

The actual effect of the suspension was minimal. Teams kept playing, and classes kept functioning. Butler President Robert Aley called it a "technical offense." Some Butler graduates who wanted to teach had to get special approval, however. About a hundred school districts in Indiana were members of the association, and the rules called for such a procedure in order to teach in a member school

For a while it appeared that Clark would stay on at Butler. He held spring football practice and seemed to be proceeding with the program. But in August 1930 the *Indianapolis Star* announced Clark's resignation and stated that it was "believed linked to suspension of the school by the North Central Association." A few days later it was announced that the athletic director at Lombard College in Galesburg, Illinois, Harry Bell, would succeed Clark.

Reinstatement by the association was granted one year to the day after it suspended the university. Butler's endowment meantime had been increased to five million dollars, faculty had been added, and books in the library had been increased by 50 percent.

The suspension occurred right after Hinkle had experienced

a disappointing basketball season. He had had high hopes for the 1929–30 team. It was built around five returning veterans of his national championship squad, plus a junior, Cleon Reynolds. Things worked at first. It won eight of its first nine games. Purdue, with two all-Americans in John Wooden and Charles (Stretch) Murphy, won the Big Ten championship and lost only two games all year, one to Butler. Other early season Bulldog victims included Illinois, Chicago, Vanderbilt, and Nebraska. Then disaster struck.

Team captain Hildebrand was ruled ineligible. It was determined he had received money for playing on a baseball team the previous summer in Brazil, Indiana. The days of looking the other way over that activity were gone. Hosier graduated at mid-year, Hubert Hinchman was lost because of illness, and Richard Wolfe lost because of ineligibility. Butler won only three more games.

Marshall Tackett, from Martinsville High School where he had been a teammate of Wooden's, and Lyle Withrow were the only letter winners that year who earned awards the next year. But the 1930–31 team, with such new faces as Ray Miller, Howard Chadd, and Searle Proffit, clicked. The team went 17–2, and the season ended with a come-from-behind win over Notre Dame in the fieldhouse.

At the end of the season the *Indianapolis Star* reported rumors that the University of Michigan was interested in hiring Hinkle. That was several years before Hinkle's old friend Fritz Crisler revived the football program there and twice approached Hinkle about heading the basketball program. Hinkle didn't leave, of course; something may have told him he might be getting some of his old jobs back.

The new football coach, Bell, managed only two wins his first year, 1930. When Hinkle's sixth basketball team (1931–32) opened its season with a veteran group and a win over Evansville at the fieldhouse, Bell had won only three more. Bell resigned by January, and Hinkle was renamed athletic director but not football coach. The head grid coach at Ohio Wesleyan, Fred Mackey, got that job. Hinkle, now the boss, immediately resumed his old job as baseball coach.

That was after he had guided the basketball team to a 14–5 season, adding Southern California, Pittsburgh, and Illinois to his conquest list. Some familiar names were on that 1931–32 team. Frank Baird became the long-time coach and athletic director at Broad Ripple High School. Searle Proffit became director of the athletic program at Wiley High School in Terre Haute, and Frank Reissner became a prominent Indianapolis businessman and Butler loyalist.

Butler's fifth football coach in twelve years had a brief career. Mackey could manage only four wins in the two seasons he labored at the job. Injuries made it difficult the first season, and no one knows how much a de-emphasis on football in the post–Potsy Clark days affected the program. At any rate, Mackey was removed and Hinkle got another old job back, assigned to be the football coach effective with the 1934 season.

Hinkle had added two more successful basketball seasons when he got the word. With Proffit and Miller as co-captains, the 1932–33 squad won sixteen of twenty-one games. The school had become a member of the Missouri Valley Conference and Butler dominated it, winning the title with only one loss. Members besides Butler were Drake, Grinnell, Oklahoma A & M (with its own legendary coach, Henry Iba), Creighton, and Washington of St. Louis. That Butler team split with Notre Dame, winning at South Bend and losing an overtime thriller at the fieldhouse before a crowd of ten thousand. All-American center Moose Krause headed for the Basketball Hall of Fame and a long career as Notre Dame athletic director, scored eighteen points and got one basket while lying on the floor.

Many years later at a testimonial for Krause in Indianapolis, Hinkle was one of the roasters. He could always do that well. Hinkle said that the only way to beat Notre Dame when Krause was playing was to foul him, "so we fouled him thirty times in one game at Notre Dame and he made only five." Krause rebutted by saying it was really six.

In the 1933–34 season with Baird as captain, Butler repeated as Missouri Valley champions and won fourteen of twenty-one. Now the pattern was set. Tony Hinkle was in charge as athletic director and was coaching not one, not two, but three sports. It was a combination he found irresistible. With the exception of the World War II period, which brought a temporary alteration, that was the way he would operate the program to the end in 1970.

8 Early Football Years

Hinkle's second debut as head football coach, in 1934, was memorable for two reasons: (1) his team scored a thrilling season-opening victory but (2) few saw it because, as an *Indianapolis Star* writer expressed it, "practically the entire game was played in a drizzling rain or a blinding downpour." Most of the crowd either stayed home, departed early, or sought refuge in the fieldhouse.

The game was highly publicized in advance, and ladies were admitted free. Kickoff was 8:15 P.M. (Butler had been playing most of its September-October home games since 1930 under a newly installed lighting system.) Ball State Teachers College, as it was then known, was the opponent. Those who peered through the deluge reported that the ball was difficult to handle and fumbles resulted. Twice the Bulldogs found the visitors deep in their own territory as a result. Ball State scored two safeties in the second quarter and led 4–0 at halftime. In the second half Butler twice blocked kicks to set up situations that produced touchdowns and a win, 13–4.

Tony, now with Wally Middlesworth back as assistant coach and with some sophomores playing key roles, directed that team to a 6–1–1 season and the state's secondary college football title.

Long-time basketball opponent and friend Ed Krause presents a Notre Dame blanket to Tony Hinkle in ceremonies just moments before Hinkle coached his last Butler University basketball game in 1970. Krause is behind the podium. At left, standing beside Hinkle, are members of his family. Seated next to the podium (left to right) are master of ceremonies Tom Carnegie, Indianapolis Mayor Richard Lugar, Indiana Governor Edgar Whitcomb, and Butler President Alexander Jones.

Tony Hinkle, one of only three men in the history of the University of Chicago to receive nine athletic letters, was an end on the football team, a guard in basketball, and pitcher-outfielder in baseball. Freshmen were not allowed to play on varsity teams.

Butler's big fieldhouse opened in 1928, seven years after Tony Hinkle took his athletic fortunes to Butler University in Indianapolis, and it aroused the interest of basketball coaches throughout the country.

Paul Daniel Hinkle was probably two years old when this picture was taken at his birthplace, his grandparents' farm near Logansport, Indiana. At left is his mother's father, Daniel Ray, the source of the future coach's middle name. To the right are his parents, Edgar and Winnie.

(*Above, left*) Edgar Hinkle's childhood had little or no home life, but he grew to be a highly motivated educator in Chicago and a devoted husband and father.

(*Above, right*) Winnie Ray Hinkle was the product of loving parents who could provide her with far more comforts than Edgar had ever known. She was a devoted wife and mother whose three children were born over a span of twenty-four years. Paul was the oldest.

(*Left*) Paul was approaching his eleventh birthday when baby sister Florence arrived. Florence adored her big brother, who was quite willing to take the blame when she did something wrong.

Amos Alonzo Stagg established a program at the University of Chicago that brought the school into athletic prominence. Stagg produced awe, respect, and even fear in those like Tony Hinkle who played for him.

The famed Stagg Field was removed from the University of Chicago campus many years ago, replaced in part by a large library. But the fieldhouse (to the right of the field) used in Tony's time for basketball still stood in 1990.

Tony Hinkle, holding the basketball front row center, captained the Chicago basketball team that won the Big Ten championship in 1919–20. Hinkle's friend Fritz Crisler is second from left in the front row. Coach Pat Page, who moved to Butler a few months later and eventually hired Hinkle as his assistant, is at extreme left in the second row.

Fritz Crisler (left) was a year behind Hinkle in school. The two friends became starting guards in basketball and starting ends in football. Crisler went on to establish a powerful football program at the University of Michigan and twice tried to convince Tony he should be that school's basketball coach.

Irwin Field was considered quite adequate for football when Hinkle arrived at Butler in the early 1920s and became, among other things, the school's assistant football coach. This photo was taken during a game with DePauw in 1923, when the Butler campus was on Indianapolis's eastside in Irvington.

The third Butler basketball team coached by Tony Hinkle (1928–29) was declared national collegiate champion. This picture appeared in the 1929 *Drift,* the Butler yearbook. First row (left to right): Maurice Hosier, Alan Fromuth, Frank White, Dana Chandler, Jacob Caskey; second row: trainer Willie McGill, Marshall Christopher, Wilbur Allen, Oral Hildebrand, Cleon Reynolds, assistant coach Bob Nipper; third row: student manager George Lloyd, Hinkle, William Bugg, graduate manager Ralph Hitch, assistant coach Archie Chadd. The team record was 17–2.

True, the schedule had been trimmed down. Gone were such powers as Notre Dame, Minnesota, Illinois, and Purdue. But they had been off the schedule since 1930, and the coaches in the interim still had had only mild success.

One member of that 1934 team, Paul Moore, had grown up in a rural area of the state and went to Butler after an alumnus spotted him at the age of eighteen assisting a mechanic at a public garage out in the country. He had made all-state honorable mention as a high school player but hadn't even thought of going to college, primarily because of costs. The visitor told Paul that he had just graduated and that his job serving food and clearing tables (probably at a fraternity house) was open. Two weeks later, the visitor and five other alumni returned to talk to Moore. Then, as Moore recalled in 1989, "My mom got my two shirts and suit of underwear and spare pants, stuffed them in a bag, and I went to Butler."

Moore first played for Hinkle when Hinkle was freshman coach in 1931. At one point, he said, he was convinced he had made a mistake in going to Butler and told "Hink" he was going home. Hinkle's words probably changed the course of his life: "I think I understand, but if you bear out this first year you can make it from then on. When you get out of school and you are a college man you will be a lot better off than if you go home in the country and shuck corn or something like that." In 1934 Moore played guard for Hinkle as a senior second stringer. He graduated with a degree in business. Later in life he decided to earn a law degree and recently retired from practicing law.

That was the kind of thing that happened at Butler at that time as the area struggled with the effects of the Depression. Alumni were recruiting spontaneously, and Hinkle found time to listen to players and provide encouragement.

Tony's football program continued to prosper. He led his team to several so-called secondary college championships—the Indiana Intercollegiate Conference in the 1930s embraced every college and university in the state except Notre Dame, Purdue, and Indiana. It was 1941 before a Hinkle-coached football team lost to a state conference team (St. Joseph's). For eight years Tony didn't have a losing season, and twice, 1936 and 1939, his teams were undefeated.

That is not to say that the program was free of problems. There was also personal tragedy. Hinkle and his assistant, Middlesworth, were having dinner at a downtown hotel, no doubt discussing their team's big win over Valparaiso that afternoon in the Bowl, when they got the news. The team's popular captain and quarterback, Spero Costas, had been killed near Crawfordsville in an automobile accident. The car had gone out of control and hit a tree. Police believed it had been driven at excessive speed. Costas was a passenger along with star halfback Inman Blackaby. Blackaby was released from the hospital after treatment for his injuries. Two others were injured critically. The *Indianapolis Star* stated that Costas had been "rated by many Indiana sports writers as one of the best passers and blocking backs in Indiana collegiate circles." The coaches went immediately to the Crawfordsville hospital to be with their players and meet with the parents.

Then, only twenty-four hours later, they learned that the player chosen to be captain of the 1936–37 basketball team, Arthur Cosgrove, was near death, the victim of an automobile crash on the near northside of Indianapolis. Cosgrove survived. He didn't play basketball that year but returned to captain the 1937–38 team.

No one can recreate Hinkle's handling of these unexpected circumstances, but somehow he got his team together for the season-ending football game at Kalamazoo, Michigan. The team came through in the closing minutes, coming from behind to win over Western State (now Western Michigan), 13–7. The win produced the school's first undefeated season since 1908. There were two ties. One of them was with the University of Chicago, and it was the last time Hinkle was involved in a football game on his old home turf, Stagg Field. In the need for somebody special to address the football banquet that year, Tony's old friend Fritz Crisler fit the role. He then was the head football coach at Princeton.

Three years later, in 1939, another member of a Butler football team was seriously injured in a head-on collision near Bluffton. Right halfback Frank Celerek was traveling with a member of the basketball team, Lyle Neat, who was less seriously injured. Earlier that evening Celerek had been in the lineup when the team came from behind in another one of those rain-filled night contests at the Bowl to beat Ohio University, 12–7. Stan Crawford had blocked two punts to set up the touchdowns, the last one by senior back Tom Harding in the final seconds of the game.

Harding also had a special role in Butler history. More than once through the years Hinkle referred to Harding as perhaps his most talented athlete. But right in the middle of his Butler career, a school opponent refused to allow him to play. He was black.

Harding credited freshman coach Frank (Pop) Heddon for encouraging him to enroll at Butler. By then Hinkle had numerous graduates coaching in high schools, forming an effective recruiting network. Heddon coordinated it. Heddon's good natured personality fitted perfectly in preparing incoming students, many from rural areas, to adjust to life as college athletes. Harding had surfaced at Crispus Attucks, Indianapolis's all-black high school. His speed got him moved from the line to the backfield in football. He also excelled as a sprinter in track and as an outfielder in baseball. But he didn't go immediately to Butler. He enrolled at a school for blacks, Morehouse College in Atlanta. Heddon apparently got word that Harding was not happy there and contacted him. He assured him that, like many other players, he could earn enough money from jobs at Butler to cover the school's tuition and book costs. Butler offered no athletic scholarships; needy team members earned their way through such jobs as maintenance of the fieldhouse and waiting tables.

Harding's sophomore year was 1937. He started as a substitute in the backfield and by the fourth game of the season was at left half, sharing time with the senior captain, Blackaby. By 1938 Harding was leading the Bulldog attack. After an impressive game against Purdue in the Bowl, the team had a game scheduled in Washington, D.C., with George Washington University.

A few hours before the train was to leave Hinkle met with Harding. He had received a telegram from George Washington University refusing to play Butler if Harding was allowed on the field. Tony told Harding he would cancel the game if he wanted him to. Harding said he thought the teams should play and that maybe someone would note the irony: a university in the nation's capital city was rejecting him because of the color of his skin. Harding accompanied his team and walked on the field in street clothes to sit on the bench. Later he recalled that his reception was a chorus of boos and abusive language from the crowd. The Colonials won that game, 26–0.

The following year the Bulldogs had another undefeated season. The sweetest victory for Hinkle and Harding came the day the George Washington team showed up at the Bowl. Harding scored both of Butler's touchdowns, scampering seventy-two yards for the second one before an approving crowd.

Harding won eight varsity letters at Butler. Besides the three for football, there were two in track and three in baseball, where he was a strong hitter and most effective center fielder. Professional baseball scouts were intrigued, and more than one turned up to observe Harding. But this was six years before America's national pastime truly became national, its racial barrier falling with Jackie Robinson, a college star himself at UCLA during Harding's Butler years. Oddly, baseball was open to Latins but not to American blacks. One organization offered to sign Harding up and send him to Cuba first to play. They could get better acceptance by bringing him into their program as a Cuban. Harding said no thanks. Hinkle said Harding was perfectly capable of predating Robinson as the first black in the major leagues. He became a long-time faculty member at Crispus Attucks.

James Hauss, who joined the football coaching staff in time for the 1938 season when Harding was playing, noted how much Hinkle stressed fundamentals of the game, just as he did in basketball. Hauss was in charge of the middle linemen, Middlesworth tended to the backfield, and Hinkle concentrated on the quarterbacks and ends. Hinkle generally left the decision making to his assistants but sometimes put out subtle hints. Hauss said that if Hinkle asked how so-and-so was doing, he knew Hinkle had already decided on a replacement.

That subtlety could extend to players, too. Hauss remembered Hinkle's technique for bringing a backfield man back to reality from too much newspaper praise. During a practice scrimmage, Hinkle would put the word out to the linemen to let the opposition come through a few times. Then Hinkle would go over to his "target" and ask him what was wrong, since he'd been reading so much about how good he was. At that point, the youngster would respond that he wasn't getting any blocking protection. Hinkle would then exclaim loudly for all backfield men to hear: "Oh, it takes blocking to make it all work, does it?"

Hinkle learned the game of football from a master in the sport, but his education was rounded out by friendship with another legendary coach, Notre Dame's Rockne. Tony first met Rockne when he and his University of Chicago teammates went to South Bend to play the Irish in baseball. The game was rained out and to the visitors' delight, Rockne joined them at a nearby restaurant.

Their paths crossed more and more after Tony went to Butler and began attending coaches' meetings. They conversed frequently, and more times than not Hinkle was the listener. But there was one shining exception. As the two were traveling back to Indiana on a train following a meeting in Nebraska, Rockne asked for a little advice and Tony was ready with a suggestion. He said he had noticed that Notre Dame always shifted to the right before running a particular play. Hinkle suggested a reverse from time to time to get a crack at the opponent's weak side. Rockne incorporated the suggestion and used it with success. Only a few years later Tony lost his confidante when Rockne was killed in a plane crash.

Many lasting friendships grow up between a coach and his players, and probably no coach had more long-term friendships than Hinkle. In 1940 Hinkle's football captain was Joe Dezelan. The night before the homecoming game with DePauw, Dezelan quit the team and dropped out of school. He blamed "business conditions and scholastic difficulties" for the decision. Joe joined up with his two brothers who were operating a bowling alley. Four years later Cathedral High School was looking for a football coach. Dezelan wanted the job, and the school made a deal with him: if he would start working toward finishing his schooling, he could have the job immediately. Dezelan earned his degree at Butler and coached football the next twenty-six seasons. In the process he wrote to his old coach, who was then in the navy, and asked for any suggestions he might have. Hinkle wished him well, provided some advice, and diagrammed two plays for him. Over the next twenty-six years, Dezelan became to Cathedral and Indianapolis football the kind of giant Hinkle was for Butler. In 1979 Cathedral presented Hinkle with a special scroll from "Hink's Kids." It listed more than a hundred Cathedral graduates who had played for Hinkle in football, basketball, and baseball.

9 The Hinkle System

Tony Hinkle's basketball offensive strategy—"the Hinkle system," it grew to be known—started taking shape at the University of Chicago. It evolved slowly in the 1920s and began to blossom at Butler in the 1930s. Herbert Schwomeyer, who played for Hinkle and served him as an assistant, explained it as constant movement of the ball between pairs of players. Tony had worked out an array of fourteen two-man exercises designed to block out defensive players; today they are known as picks and screens.

The system concentrated on getting good percentage shots, since most opponents were bigger than Butler and Tony never counted on getting the ball back on a rebound. When asked his description of the strategy in a few words, Bob Dietz answered: "It was a system of basketball where everybody moved, everybody got to handle the ball, everybody got to shoot. Some shoot more than others [looking for their own good percentage shot]. . . . Everybody has a place to go and the ball keeps moving."

The technique also called for constant repetition exercised through drills. Player after player has said that the offensive drill on the first day of practice with Hinkle was identical to the offensive drill on the final day of practice. Hinkle wanted habits so deeply ingrained in his players that they would respond to changing situations without thinking. Their actions were to come through a programmed response.

The Hinkle system didn't have the flash and dash of what Ward (Piggy) Lambert was doing at Purdue with the fast break. But neither was it the slow, deliberate style many teams used in the 1920s and 1930s when they had to fight a tall center after each field goal to get possession of the ball. As John Wooden put it, Hinkle's teams "were always looking for the shot." There was "always a lot of movement in his game. The men knew where they were to go and how to get there." Wooden said it was "nothing like the slow, control style they were playing on the West Coast in the 1930s and 1940s at all."

A similar offense was being used at the University of Pittsburgh. During the 1920s and 1930s hardly a season went by that didn't see Hinkle and Pitt coach Doc Carlson match teams and strategies. In those games Hinkle teams came out ahead, six wins to five.

There was nothing secret about the Hinkle system. In fact, Hinkle took selected players with him to explain it at clinics. These clinics sometimes doubled as vacation breaks. Hinkle once took his wife and two young daughters with him to a clinic at Daytona Beach along with some assistants and players. But learning about the system directly from its formulator and implementing it properly were two different matters. Schwomeyer recalled a good example of that: "He taught it so much better than anybody else could teach it that he could tell you what he was going to do, and then beat you doing it. I sat from about eleven o'clock one night until about a quarter to three with him, while he explained and outlined his system to an opposing coach. Three weeks later, they came down to play us and we beat 'em."

It was a magical time for Hinkle and his basketball program. Coaches of major schools wanted to be on his schedule and youngsters wanted to play for him. Most of the time the talent coming out of Indiana high schools more than filled the bill. Frank Baird is an example. Baird grew up on the eastside of Indianapolis. His main interest was baseball. As a kid he watched Hinkle's teams in Irvington and then at the new campus. He learned basketball at Arsenal Technical High School. A top student, he turned down a scholarship to DePauw because he wanted to play for Hinkle. A walkon who didn't even get a job to work off part of his tuition, Baird earned three letters in baseball and three in basketball. He captained the 1933–34 basketball team and was named to an all-American team. He went on to a teaching career at Broad Ripple High School of more than forty years; many of those years he was the baseball and basketball coach.

Butler ended its brief two-year basketball participation in the Missouri Valley Conference in 1934. The administration declared that travel was too costly. What it didn't say was that Butler would be free to find better opponents. But hard times arrived. After a 13–7 season in 1934–35, the Bulldogs won only six games in each of the next two seasons, the first losing years for Hinkle in basketball, and they went 11–12 in 1937–38.

A sophomore on that 1937–38 team who stood only five feet seven inches tall gave promise of things to come, though. Jerry Steiner, in the final game at home against Franklin, dribbled the length of the floor to score and win the game for Butler in the final seconds. Steiner was the first of a series of little men who could move and score under Hinkle. Recent rules changes had helped the smaller players. Now no one on offense could remain in the foul lane more than three seconds, and the center jump after every field goal had been eliminated. No longer could a defender touch the basket while the ball was on the rim. And a requirement that the offensive team must get the ball across midcourt within ten seconds had been put into effect.

Dietz joined Steiner on the 1938–39 team, which won fourteen of twenty games (with Iowa, Wisconsin, Michigan State, and DePaul among the victims). The big win came at the end in the fieldhouse over Notre Dame, 35–27.

The next season things got even better. Captained by Steiner, the team went 17–6. Two days before Christmas a jammed fieldhouse saw Indiana University come from behind to stop the Bulldogs, 40–33. (Branch McCracken's Hoosiers finished that season by winning the recently established National Collegiate Athletic Association tournament.) Tony took his team to Madison Square Garden right after New Year's to do battle with a highly regarded Long Island University team, coached by Clair Bee. Butler fell behind early, then made a gallant comeback in the second half before losing. The *New York Times* was impressed: "The Bulldogs never despaired, but kept hustling with might and main. They did not have size but they had plenty of spirit. . . . The eye-catching performer was Jerry Steiner of Butler, the smallest man on the floor. He was a streak and became the game's high man with 15 points, while Dietz, a one hand specialist, had 14." Two days later, playing in Convention Hall in Philadelphia, the team beat La Salle by nine points and Steiner scored twenty-two.

Years afterward, Steiner choked up when he talked about that trip. The youngster from Berne, Indiana, had never been on a train before. When the team returned to Indianapolis about nine o'clock in the evening, the Butler band and a substantial number of students were waiting to greet them at Union Station. Steiner recalled that during the return trip, his coach sat down beside him and said simply, "You had a pretty good trip, kid." It was the understatement of the season.

The team closed out its season with a hectic win over old rival Notre Dame, 39–38. It was the team's seventeenth victory, and Hinkle had his program on a roll again. Steiner was named to Madison Square Garden's all-American quintet.

The next season, with Dietz as captain, it was up and down but there were some stimulating moments. The season opener was with NCAA champion Indiana University at the fieldhouse;

the Hoosiers won by three points with a late rally. Twice Butler beat Ohio State, and there was a fourteen-point win over Notre Dame with Dietz leading the scoring. For the second straight year the team traveled east, but this time it went 0–2 at the Garden and in Philadelphia. Hinkle summed it up at the basketball banquet that year when he noted that "this year's team played some of the best ball ever played by a Butler team—and some of the worst." Dietz broke the three-year scoring record previously held by Hildebrand.

Hinkle's last pre–World War II team opened its season the night before Pearl Harbor, with a win over Franklin at the fieldhouse. By the time the season was over Hinkle was packing his bags for military service, and so were other key members of the coaching staff. Hinkle had completed sixteen seasons of Butler basketball with only three losing seasons and schedules that included some of the best competition available at the time.

10 Home Life and Hoosier Hysteria

Success at Butler Fieldhouse, in Butler Bowl, and on the baseball diamond wasn't all that enhanced Tony's life in the 1930s. He and Jane became parents twice during the early part of that decade. Daughter Barbara arrived first, and Patricia followed less than a year and a half later. They soon learned that their father had a far different schedule than most dads.

During football and basketball seasons especially, Hinkle was away from home many evenings, and on weekends there were meetings with coaches and discussions about films the girls didn't much understand. Sometimes late on Sunday afternoons their dad met with his coaching staff at the home the Hinkles acquired during the 1930s at 415 West 46th Street. At these Sunday gatherings, Jane would provide snacks and soft drinks.

The girls grew to appreciate their dad, who at rare moments joked and laughed with them but more times than not was thinking about the next game or reassessing the last loss and how it could be avoided the next time. Patricia recalled that Sundays got to be one of their favorite days. As they grew a little older, their dad would take them to the fieldhouse, where he would let them help the athletes pick up the debris left by the

Saturday crowd while he went to his office to study statistics and plan his week ahead.

Needless to say, the daughters during this period were closer to their mother and their grandmother (Jane's mother lived with family for a number of years). Both have said laughingly that they think their dad would have been more comfortable with sons, agreeing that he wasn't always at ease around women. A close family friend said that Tony was at a loss to deal with the concerns of daughters and just didn't know how to handle them.

Sometimes when Dad was home, the girls learned, there were moments when you kept your distance. It wasn't fear. It was the knowledge that he was analyzing a loss. Patricia, known to her friends as Patty (now Mrs. David Watson), described one of those late evenings: "He'd get very quiet. He wouldn't get mad or anything. He just wouldn't talk. He'd just sit and stare and think. Then he'd be up early the next morning looking at the pictures."

That was the Hinkle style. It was complete absorption in what he enjoyed doing most. And once again he was put to the test of deciding whether the best place for him to do it was Butler. In the mid-1930s he was offered the athletic directorship at Lafayette College in Easton, Pennsylvania. The school wanted him to run the department but not coach. The administration wanted to pay him six thousand dollars a year, probably more than he was drawing at Butler. He declined the offer.

In the fall of 1939 Tony signed a new three-year contract. Although the terms were not disclosed the Board of Trustees issued a statement:

> The Board appreciates the fact that Mr. Hinkle has won the respect, admiration and affection of not only the athletes but the student body, alumni and friends of the institution. It is our hope that he will remain as director of athletics at Butler University for many years to come.

It was during this same period that Tony struck up a friendship with the sports editor of the *Indianapolis News*, William Fox, Jr. Fox had joined the newspaper just a few months before Hinkle went to Butler. They were very different people but the combination clicked. Fox not only wrote about sports; he also injected poetry and quotations from classical literature into his reports. Hinkle provided Fox with the insights and experiences of an athlete and coach. Fox is credited with coining the phrase "Hoosier hysteria" in a highly popular high school basketball column called "Shootin' Em Stoppin' Em." The *News* always claimed (and it would be difficult to dispute) that Fox "more than any other person . . . was responsible for making high school basketball Indiana's leading sport."

Through 1935, the one-class state tournament played down to a "Sweet Sixteen" group of teams that would get together for a championship showdown at Butler Fieldhouse. Regional tournaments determined the finalists, and after the regionals, Fox and Hinkle would get in a car and visit each of the schools. Fox would write his stories at night, long after Hinkle had gone to sleep. Then Fox would make up for it with naps in the car while Hinkle drove to the next stop. Even after the tournament format changed to a Final Four concept (the NCAA was to use the pattern a decade later) Fox and Hinkle were a familiar pair in basketball hamlets throughout the state.

At some point, probably in the early 1930s, Hinkle took on an additional responsibility at the fieldhouse: the concessions. Although there was talk at the time that he was getting a percentage of what he sold, there is no evidence of it. There are those who recall seeing Hinkle busily handling chores behind a counter during the off season when the fieldhouse was used for a number of other events. The concessions business also apparently provided additional tuition jobs for athletes.

One of the biggest events at the fieldhouse besides the basketball games was the Butler Relays. Track and field competition had never been high on Hinkle's wish list. He always enthusiastically turned to baseball once the basketball season ended. But when the Butler track coach Hermon Phillips, a former NCAA 440-yard champion for Butler and a 1928 Olympian, came to him with an idea in the early 1930s about establishing an indoor track and field meet that would attract top collegiate athletes, Tony listened and supported him.

Phillips and Hinkle laid out the proposal to Butler President James Putnam, who promptly said no because of the expense. He also feared the games would lose money and cause financial harm. Without hesitation, Hinkle and Phillips pledged they personally would make up any losses to the university. One wonders how they would have managed that if it had been necessary. It wasn't; the Butler Relays proved to be a huge success.

The first event was held in March 1933 with sixteen schools participating. Among them were five Big Ten teams including talented teams from Indiana University, Michigan, and Illinois. The fieldhouse was filled to capacity. However, seating had to be reduced. All lower bleachers were removed and part of that space was used for box seats at premium prices. Those in the boxes wore formal attire, as did all the officials. Indianapolis merchants cooperated by sponsoring the twelve events. Ohio State's Jesse Owens tied the world record in the sixty-yard dash in the 1935 Relays and was one-tenth of a second away from another tie. It was a year before he would compete for the United States in the 1936 Olympics in Munich, Germany. The Relays remained a popular annual event at Butler for ten years and never lost money. Hinkle was heavily involved in staging the event.

During the prewar period many of the athletes who showed up to play at Butler couldn't afford the costs of school. They survived by working at jobs that provided credit toward tuition debts. They usually had an additional job or two to cover other matters. Out-of-towners needed places to sleep. Those in town lived at home and operated by streetcars or buses.

A typical out-of-town Butler athlete was Jim Hauss. He came from the small community of Chili (pronounced chye-lye) in north central Indiana, too far to commute. Freshman coach Heddon coordinated his "economic survival" plan. Hauss was assigned to the cleanup maintenance crew at the fieldhouse. That was worth 27.5 cents an hour, which was credited toward his tuition. His living arrangement was the basement of a private home near campus his entire college career. That cost was met by firing the furnace and cleaning the house on Saturdays. His meals were provided at the Delta Gamma sorority house, where he worked as a house boy. That meant washing dishes during the day and waiting tables in the evening. All that was scheduled around a full load of classes and football practices. Hauss went to Butler to play basketball. When Heddon and Tony saw his size they told him he should play football. He learned the game well, lettered two years, and served as head line coach for over thirty years. He never did earn his letter in basketball.

Heddon played a key role in coordinating the financial matters of athletes Hinkle wanted while running the freshman programs in both football and basketball. He had assumed that position when Bob Nipper left to become football coach at Shortridge High School. Heddon became "Pop" to Butler athletes, partly because of his tendency toward baldness and partly because many of the out-of-towners considered him a sort of part-time father. Pop's gregarious personality was just right to prepare them for the more reserved, more subtle Hinkle.

Heddon also was the school's primary recruiter during the prewar years. He was always on the lookout for prospects in and around Indianapolis and sometimes in far-off places, as in the case of Tom Harding at Morehead. It is said that one of his favorite basketball lookout points was the Dearborn Gymnasium on East Michigan and the Pennsy Gym just south of Willard Park, favorite gathering spots for youngsters who were eager to play the game.

In 1942 Heddon suddenly found himself in charge. Hinkle, Hauss, Middlesworth, and the athletic trainer, James Morris, departed for military service. Hinkle had accepted the post of athletic instructor at the big Great Lakes Naval Training Center north of Chicago.

Hinkle's youthful coaching years at Butler had come to an end. He would never be quite the same again. When he returned he would be approaching age forty-seven and have an added background of coaching that brought him in contact with some of the finest athletes of the time. He would be more confident than ever and be looked upon by his athletes as "the old man," as he once viewed Stagg. But there would be a major difference. Hinkle would wear a perpetual scowl, but his mind would be full of fun. After the war he would use the combination effectively, sometimes with sarcasm, to make his point in correcting a flaw in one of his kids' techniques. He would begin to take on the aura of a "character," a colorful one who could needle, be blunt, and be forceful as the occasion demanded.

Hinkle also would discover something else. He liked running the show at Butler. He thrived on coaching three sports, heading the department while still handling teaching chores. And though he never was one to command power or pursue it, he had it at Butler by his very presence and by the jobs he performed. His experience in the U.S. Navy would be useful and his contribution significant, but it wouldn't lead him away from Butler.

11 Navy Years

For a few weeks it looked as if Tony was going to rejoin his old teammate from the University of Chicago, Fritz Crisler, at Great Lakes. Crisler had established himself as an extremely successful football coach, first at Minnesota, then at Princeton, and for the past four seasons at Michigan. The navy wanted Crisler to handle football and Hinkle basketball. Crisler was beyond draft age (as was Tony), and Tony suspected that Fritz wanted a higher rank than the navy was offering. Tony accepted the commission, lieutenant. Fritz declined, and the navy decided to let Hinkle coach the football team too.

While his commission was clearing navy red tape, Hinkle went ahead and reported for duty as a civilian. He was on the base in time to assist in coaching the last four basketball games of the 1941–42 season. Then, just as he did at Butler, he moved to baseball. The manager of the Great Lakes team was a former Detroit Tiger star, Mickey Cochrane. Hinkle assisted, along with Indiana University athlete Emil Andres. Twice Tony headed back on weekends to attend to things at Butler. Once was for the Butler Relays, the other was for the state high school basketball finals.

Ironically, Hinkle's first gridiron test as coach of the Bluejackets, as the service team was known, was against Crisler's Michigan eleven at Ann Arbor. The sailors, sporting players from over thirty universities in addition to some professional clubs, were upset that September afternoon in 1942, 9–0. In fact, Tony's team won only two of its first five games. A United Press staff correspondent, Tommy Devine, wrote that "Hinkle's outfit has been the flop of the current gridiron season, yet public criticism of him or the team has been slight. The football writing gentry has taken a tolerant attitude and the Bluejackets have been given the benefit of every doubt."

Actually, it looked a lot easier than it was. The team had to be molded in a little over three weeks and practically everyone was unfamiliar with fellow team members. Hinkle also found that those with professional experience had less enthusiasm for hard workouts than the ones who had been playing in college. The navy offered the gridders few favors. Reveille was at 5:30 A.M., and they were expected to put in a full day's work, then report to practice at 4 P.M. when liberty began. Practice time was limited to one hour.

After that slow 2–5 start, Hinkle's ability to get results began to show. The team experienced no more losses and was named by sports writers as the country's best military service football team. It played all its games on the road that season, prevailing over Missouri, Purdue, Marquette, and Illinois following earlier victories over Iowa and Pittsburgh. The final game of the season was at Soldiers Field in Chicago, where thirty-five thousand frigid fans watched Notre Dame quarterback Angelo Bertelli, two years before he would win the Heisman trophy, hold the sailors to a 13–13 tie.

Bob Dietz once remarked that Hinkle suddenly had the best recruiting program one could imagine backing him. In fact, Dietz was assigned to play basketball for his old coach along with another Butler graduate, Wilber Schumacher. They both contributed to the team's considerable scoring abilities. There were some other familiar names on the team. They included Forrest (Fordy) Anderson from Gary Emerson High School and Stanford, later a great college coach himself; Bob Davies, a future Hall of Fame player from Seton Hall, on his way to a great and long professional career; and Pete Newell, who would have a Hall of Fame coaching career. The nineteen-man roster contained lots of talent, though it was not particularly tall. The tallest player was George Glamack from North Carolina, at six feet four.

Hinkle's basketball team played thirty-seven games in a little over three months with trips limited to the Midwest. The navy used the team for a double purpose—recruiting and morale. The morale came at the base where the team made fourteen appearances. The team won all but three games against a variety of college teams, both large and small. Universities with certain navy academic programs such as V-12 allowed their athletes to compete on their school's teams. The army, on the other hand, forbade such participation. Thus the big schools with the right navy programs provided the strongest opposition. The only defeats came from Illinois, Northwestern and Notre Dame. The latter game went to overtime, the season finale at Great Lakes, and broke a twenty-four-game winning streak.

Hinkle's daughters, Barbara and Patty, remembered the two years or so they lived at Great Lakes differently, at least where their father was concerned. Barbara recalled seeing more of their dad than had been the custom at Butler. Patty said nothing really changed, that their father was just as absorbed in what he was doing in the navy as he had been at Butler. But both agreed that they liked the excitement of navy living. Both attended schools nearby, at Lake Forest and Lake Bluff, Illinois.

In the fall of 1943 it was a whole new football group for Hinkle. Athletes were allowed only one year of duty on Great Lakes teams during the war. The college graduates received commissions. Many were assigned overseas duty. The Great Lakes roster that year included Emil (Red) Sitko, a Fort Wayne athlete, who had completed one year at Notre Dame. He figured in the thriller of the season, the final game with the Irish.

The Bluejackets had gone 9–2 before that final game. One of the two losses was to Purdue, 23–13. Frank Leahy's third Notre Dame team was undefeated and destined to be the top collegiate team in the nation. The sailors were considered to be three- to four-touchdown underdogs, even though the Irish had lost their Heisman Trophy winner, Angelo Bertelli, to the Marine Corps at midseason. All Leahy had left at quarterback was eighteen-year-old sophomore Johnny Lujack. However, he proved to be quite able.

The Great Lakes–Notre Dame game was to be played at Great Lakes' Ross Field (capacity twenty-two thousand) on the last Saturday in November. Notre Dame alumni put the pressure on their school's administration to get the game moved to the more spacious Soldiers Field in Chicago. When it was pointed out that many sailors would be unable to attend if the change was made, Notre Dame's president J. Hugh O'Donnell refused to challenge the scheduling. He pointed out that "navy morale" was far more important than gate receipts. Navy personnel attended at no charge.

Hinkle had a strategy whirling around in his head for that game. He told Tom Keating about it when Keating was preparing a story for the *Indianapolis Star*: "When Lujack went back to pass he had only one receiver in mind to throw to and he didn't look for anyone else. He kept his back turned to the line as he dropped back and where he looked first was where he always passed. So we gambled and played a seven-diamond defense. Notre Dame was primarily a rushing team and I thought if we could stop their ground game we might have a chance. Anyway, if it didn't work, I figured the navy couldn't fire me."

Notre Dame scored early on fourteen power plays, two short passes, and a one-yard sneak. Keating noted that when Lujack completed all four passes he tried that first quarter, Hinkle's strategy looked suspect. However, in the second quarter two of his passes were intercepted to stop scoring drives and Hinkle remained in his seven-diamond defense. Great Lakes trailed, 7–0, at halftime.

Early in the third quarter five-foot-seven halfback Sitko, who had been getting some impressive ground gains against his former school, went around left end for twenty-six yards and a touchdown. The Irish blocked the conversion attempt and still led, 7–6. On their next possession Hinkle's team scored in two plays. Former Furman star Dewey Proctor ran fifty-one yards to put the host team ahead, and the white hats in the stands were ecstatic. Once again the kick for the extra point was blocked, and the Irish were down only five, 12–7.

Leahy's team appeared to be pulling it out when they staged an eighty-yard drive in the fourth quarter that ate up time and utilized virtually every trick in Leahy's ample book of tricks. With seventy-one seconds left, using a quick count from the one-yard line, Notre Dame scored and kicked the extra point. Now the Irish appeared to have the game, 14–12.

But Hinkle still had seventy-one seconds. He made a key change. He moved former Duke star Steve Lach to quarterback because he could throw long. The regular quarterback, Paul Anderson, was moved to end. As time ran out, Lach went back to throw and found no one open. He headed for the sidelines with half the Notre Dame team chasing him. As he was tackled, he managed a pass that covered fifty-four yards into the waiting arms of Anderson, who by this time was fifteen yards behind the nearest defender. Hinkle's sailors had won, 19–14. Years later Lujack told Keating that he was in the secondary and it appeared that Lach was trapped, so he and the rest relaxed. He also agreed that the seven-diamond move was "pretty good strategy," that no one read defense much in those days.

The star throughout the game was little Sitko, who returned to Notre Dame after the war and became an all-American. Leahy would win four national championships and coach his

South Bend team to undefeated seasons that stretched from 1946 through 1949.

Five days after that highly emotional win, Hinkle was into his second and last basketball season at Great Lakes with an opening win over the Glenview Naval Air Station team. Shortly afterward, at Chicago Stadium, the team scored an impressive win over the University of Illinois "Whiz Kids," as they would be known, and a week later defeated a strong Purdue team, the first of two wins over the Boilermakers. Hinkle led the squad to a 33–3 season.

Two graduates of the highly successful Indiana University program were key factors in Hinkle's success at Great Lakes in the 1943–44 season. Herman Schaefer and Paul (Curley) Armstrong, high school teammates at Fort Wayne Central before playing on Indiana's 1940 NCAA champions, led the offense time and again. At one point during the season they were referred to as the "Hoosier Bucket Twins." Frequently one or the other or both would score well over twenty points in a game, a rarity at a time when two-handed set shots were still in vogue.

Shortly after the basketball season ended, the navy assigned Hinkle to be athletic officer at Great Lakes, a post comparable to athletic director at a university, and raised his rank to a lieutenant commander. He also got a new assistant, temporarily. Ohio State football coach Paul Brown was given a commission to succeed Hinkle as Great Lakes football coach. Navy regulations called for reassignment. However, Hinkle didn't get his orders until the football season was one game old. So for one game Brown was his assistant.

Hinkle's new job was recreation director at the U.S. naval base on Guam, one of the Mariana islands in the Pacific. The rest of the family moved back into their home in Indianapolis, joined by Jane's mother, Grace Murdock.

Hinkle was out of coaching for the first time in more than twenty-three years. But for the moment he was into something more important: morale. That had been his real purpose at

Great Lakes; it had merely shifted to the Pacific. When ships came into Guam, it was important that the crews be provided recreational facilities. Hinkle saw to it that they had them for baseball, basketball, football, movies, snacks, and drinks. In his new assignment he found many friends. Many of them had played for him or against him through the years and more recently in the military service.

Although the war in the Pacific wouldn't be over for another three months, some three hundred men from Indiana—soldiers, sailors, and marines—gathered late in April for a Hoosier reunion. This observance took place at the Turin Bay enlisted men's beach at Guam. The *Indianapolis News* war correspondent Leo Litz was there, too, and he wrote that "we had proper facilities for speech making—a loudspeaker and a toastmaster. The latter assignment had been delegated to Lt. Comdr. Paul D. (Tony) Hinkle. Tony took over at the appointed time but he didn't get very far [everyone was too busy visiting]. . . . Tony finally gave up . . . and went visiting with the Butler crowd." Lieutenant (JG) Angelo Angelopolous had assembled the Butler crowd, which numbered ten. Angelopolous, a member of the *Indianapolis News* sports staff, resumed his career there after the war.

There was never any question in Hinkle's mind about returning to Butler once life got back to normal. He said he would be back when he left, and back he went. Jane and the girls drove up to Great Lakes where he was separated from active duty. The short absences they had felt keenly when he was coaching at Butler didn't seem so bad now. Hinkle was back home with his family by the first of November.

The old fieldhouse never looked so good to him. For nearly a year during the war it had been used by the navy for a signal training school. After that it had been turned over to the U.S. Army Air Force for another school. Athletics at Butler had been greatly curtailed. By the fall of 1944 the fieldhouse had become available again, and Pop Heddon got Butler back into basketball. He and Schwomeyer had resumed the football program just before Hinkle got home.

Within two weeks Hinkle was ready to return to civilian action. He signed a contract to serve once again as athletic director and to coach football, basketball, and baseball. Twenty-five years of competition lay ahead. Within thirty days after his return his first postwar basketball team was opening the 1945–46 season at the fieldhouse.

12 Bountiful Basketball and Buckshot

Hinkle basketball returned to Butler on the first day of December, less than four months after World War II ended. Jerry Cranny, just back from service, led the team to a victory at the fieldhouse over Manchester. The Bulldogs won six of their first seven games before Louisville and Indiana University caught them. The I.U. game brought the first real crowd of the year, nine thousand, but the most fun came in January at a B-men's benefit game. A team coached by Nipper came from behind to win. On the floor that night were Hinkle, Baird, and Steiner.

It was back to the baseball diamond after that initial 12–8 basketball season ended. Chances are that Hinkle was thinking as much about football as he was about the care and treatment of the baseball facility. He got it in shape, of course. His first postwar nine went 6–6.

Football was far more difficult to get together than the other two sports. Heddon and Schwomeyer had reopened the program in 1945, but by the next year the influx of former GIs was at full tilt. There was an outpouring of students anxious to resume athletic careers that had been interrupted. Then there was the usual group, the youngsters right out of high school. One hundred thirty-six candidates reported for the first practice, by far the greatest number ever at Butler.

There wasn't enough equipment to go around. Freshman Bill Sylvester recalled that it was still difficult to buy fabric for uniforms. Coaches brought out everything they could from past seasons and put out a call for anything that might be available at warehouses in the city. Sylvester said that freshman Bill Kuntz (who would captain the 1949 team) had been practicing in tennis shoes when the assistant coach Chet McNerney noticed. "Before you come out for practice this afternoon, you get rid of those tennis shoes and put on some football shoes," McNerney said. "I go to the equipment cage after every practice and there are just no shoes available," Kuntz answered. McNerney asked him what size he needed and Kuntz told him. "Here, put these on," McNerney said, taking his own shoes off.

Some of the older members of that team, men who had earned letters before they entered service, were Knute Dobkins, Norman (Gobby) Williams, and Francis Moriarity. But youngsters contributed too, including Ott Hurle and seventeen-year-old Orville Williams, who took a pass from halfback Jim McLinn for a come-from-behind win over Indiana State, 13–7. There were twenty-five seconds left in the game when the play started from midfield.

Fans were returning to Butler Bowl. Twelve thousand turned out for a homecoming win over Ball State and nearly as many when Sylvester and Orville Williams caught touchdown passes in a victory over Wabash. The team lost only one game in 1946. And the school became a charter member of the new Mid-American Conference (MAC).

Then came the first postwar basketball dilemma. Bob Dietz was back to start his long career as Hinkle's assistant for basketball. Some two hundred candidates turned out, thirty-three of whom had earned letters in the sport at Butler. By the time football was over and Hinkle was ready to take over, Dietz had the number down to about thirty.

This team was another mixed bag of experience and age. Key freshmen who would perform the next four seasons for Hinkle were Ralph (Buckshot) O'Brien, who was five feet nine, and Jimmy Doyle. A third freshman who eventually contributed, was Marvin Wood, a mere five feet six inches tall.

Six others who would play key roles the next few seasons were McCracken rejects. All had been cut by the I.U. basketball coach, Branch McCracken. That impressive list included Charles Maas, Bob Evans, Bill Shepherd, Dee Baker, Ralph Chapman, and Bob Mehl. The tallest man for Butler was six-foot-six John Barrowcliffe, the starting center. Returnee Herod Toon was captain.

Hinkle was very aware of the two promising freshmen, O'Brien and Doyle, before they enrolled, and in that special way of his he approached them both. O'Brien remembered it this way: "I walked into Mr. Hinkle's office and he says, 'Well, son, it's nice to see you. We have a very fine school here. We do great things, educationally here. Excuse me, I've got a baseball game this afternoon. Do you mind going with me while I rake the diamond?' So I talked to him while he raked the diamond. . . . When he said he would like to have me come to Butler . . . well, he doesn't say that to many kids." Doyle said that he had been all set to go to Tulane. "But I'd grown up around Butler and had always admired Hinkle and Dietz and Steiner, all those people, so every Friday he [Hinkle] would stop by the furniture store where I worked [after he banked nearby] and we'd just talk about basketball. Finally in late August when I was ready to leave he came by and said, 'I hear you're going to Tulane,' and then he said, 'Well, you think about that because we want you at Butler and we have shoes that'll fit you.' "

Hinkle's low-key approach to recruiting was not something that just happened. It was an expression of a basic philosophy that stayed with him throughout his coaching career. No matter how competitive the search for player prospects became, Butler's coach never wanted a kid who had been talked into a commitment. He wanted the prospect to get a factual rundown of what Butler was all about and was willing to do if there was a financial need. He would push no further. He was proud of the university's academic reputation, a reputation that carried over into a strict interpretation of the rules as they pertained to athletes. In the 1940s and into the 1950s that meant Butler could continue its job program to let athletes work off tuition costs. It also was still acceptable for alumni to provide, through the university, financial help for athletes' living expenses. The athletic department could also provide team members who needed them with food tickets honored at the school cafeteria. Of course, anyone with military service got federal money through the G.I. Bill.

Lots of stories make good-natured fun of Tony's use of the word *kid* when addressing one of his athletes. There was an underlying philosophy in that, too. The coach was much more concerned with what he wanted a player to do in his overall game plan than he was in the name of each individual. His basic approach was to remind everybody that success depended on the team as a unit, not on the individual. What better way to remind them of that concept than to use the word *kid*, a number, a hometown, or an abbreviated form of the name? Max Schumacher, for instance, was "Schumie" when he was playing baseball for Hinkle.

Young O'Brien arrived with good credentials. He had led both county and city scorers in high school at Washington in Indianapolis and was named to the Indiana all-star team. His initial trip to Butler to see Hinkle had been preceded by a visit to his West New York Street home by Dietz and Hinkle, a most unusual procedure at the time. O'Brien recalled that based on those "recruiting" conversations, his goal was to make first string on the reserve team. He did, but that status changed quickly.

After a successful reserve game performance in a preliminary game at the season opener in the fieldhouse, Hinkle told O'Brien to dress for the varsity game that same night. O'Brien was ecstatic. Then Hinkle hesitated, but Buckshot finally got in with two minutes left in a loss to Wisconsin. Five nights later, old rival Pittsburgh was the opponent and substitute forward O'Brien tied Maas for scoring honors (nine points each) in a two-point win. O'Brien became a starter, permanently. One of his favorite nights that first season was the time the Hoosiers came calling. Butler beat them, and O'Brien led the scoring.

O'Brien's scoring talent (many of his points came from two-handed set shots) didn't mean that the coach kept off his back. O'Brien recalled that Hinkle was far from impressed with his defense: "He told me I had great possibilities but we were going to have to work on a few things. He told me I couldn't guard a lamppost because even the light would fake me out." Hinkle worked O'Brien on defense until he thought "my knees were going to come off."

Doyle, on the other hand, came into the program much more attuned to defensive play. But off the floor he was the shyest member of the team and vulnerable to pranks. As grim as Hinkle could appear, his sense of humor was always there lurking in the background. On a road trip, Doyle's roommate, O'Brien, found a pair of pink panties in the hotel room closet, apparently left inadvertently by a previous female occupant. Someone slipped the panties into Doyle's luggage just before checkout time. The word also was slipped to the coaching staff. When the players gathered for departure, trainer Jim Morris delivered a speech concerning complaints from the management about pilferage of towels and other materials from the rooms and stated that this was not in the tradition of Butler University. He declared a luggage check. With Hinkle looking on, it began with Doyle's bag. Jimmy turned as least as red as the panties when the coaching staff reacted in "shock." It was the type of thing that happened sooner or later with Hinkle teams.

The coach had developed the technique of never changing expressions when he was delivering a line that amused him. One night at DePauw he had benched three of his regulars, Doyle, O'Brien and Barrowcliffe, in disgust over a flat performance against the Tigers. Bill Larson was playing center and Hinkle kept yelling at him, calling him Barrowcliffe: "Damn it, Barrowcliffe, pick up the ball." Barrowcliffe was sitting right beside him and could stand it no longer. "Look, Coach, I'm not even in there and you're yelling at me." Hinkle, without any change of expression, snapped back: "Well, what the hell's the difference? If you were in there it would be the same thing."

Bill Shepherd, whose son Billy would become a "Mr. Basketball" in Indiana and be one of Hinkle's last Butler stars, knew about that Hinkle sense of humor. Bill was to be married during a Thanksgiving break. At the last preholiday practice, Tony had Shepherd going full tilt, requiring him to cut on every play. As O'Brien recalled, "he was wearing him down to his knees." Suddenly Hinkle ended it with a soulful glance at Shepherd: "Oh, I'm sorry about that. You're getting married tonight. Well, have a good night's rest."

These basketball teams of the 1940s also had fun with a new holiday event Hinkle initiated and coordinated called the Hoosier Classic. It was a two-day event at Butler Fieldhouse involving Notre Dame, Indiana, Purdue, and Butler. It was not a tournament. Butler and Notre Dame took turns playing the two Big Ten schools. The four schools divided any profits equally. Indianapolis alumni of the four schools and students in town during Christmas break responded by filling the fieldhouse. The first one was held the first two days of January 1948. The Bulldogs won five of the first six Classic games, and nearly seventy-five thousand persons attended in those first three years.

Tony's fourth postwar team (1948–49) was his best of that era. It ended its season ranked eighteenth in the nation by Associated Press. O'Brien, in his junior year, broke the Butler career scoring record.

During that season Tony took his team back to Madison Square Garden. The usual height disadvantage didn't stop them. They beat Long Island by nine points, and O'Brien scored twenty. Afterward, the team was taken to Mama Leone's well-known Manhattan restaurant. Not everyone was impressed. Marvin Wood, who had come to Butler from Morristown, a few miles southeast of Indianapolis, was heard to remark during dinner: "You know I'll be damn glad when they bring me something from the farm, so I'll know what I'm eatin'." (Wood went on to a coaching career that included a year at legendary Milan in 1954, real-life inspiration for the 1980s movie *Hoosiers*. He said he patterned his coaching after Hinkle.)

The team split with Notre Dame that season. Krause was coaching the Irish, and Leo Barnhorst from Indianapolis was the starting center. Barnhorst recalled the sort of thing Krause used to say to his teams before meeting Butler: "You're going to meet the best fundamental team you're going to play all year and you'll have to be fighting through picks and screens harder than you've done with any other team because they're so well organized. They won't be the best talent you're going to meet but they may be one of the best teams you've ever met." It was a clear definition of what Hinkle basketball was all about from an old friend and rival.

The next season, 1949–50, the team was barely above .500 when the season ended, but that didn't stop Coach William Dye of Big Ten champion Ohio State from calling Hinkle. He wanted to set up a game while his Buckeyes were awaiting the start of the NCAA tournament. The game was played in Columbus, and Butler, which had lost narrowly to OSU early in the season, almost embarrassed the Buckeyes as O'Brien broke the Ohio Coliseum individual scoring record with thirty-nine points. OSU won by one point. In the tournament it was defeated by City College of New York by one point, and CCNY went on to win the NCAA title.

Hinkle's team had come a long way since December, when their performance at Ann Arbor had been so bad in the first half that Hinkle told his team that his old friend Fritz Crisler had said some people wanted their money back. He also made them stand up, shake hands, and introduce themselves to one another because he said they were playing like people who had never played together before.

With the graduation of Doyle and O'Brien, two players Hinkle had actively recruited, a Butler basketball era was over. Doyle was second only to Buckshot in scoring and was outstanding on defense, assists, and fakes. But Tony didn't let O'Brien go without a little more fun. One afternoon in practice a man showed up in dark glasses, coat and hat pulled down low, carrying a notebook. Buckshot was told it was a man from *Look* magazine who wanted to get a look at Buckshot as he was preparing his all-American recommendations. The team went into a scrimmage and no one would pass the ball to O'Brien, who was getting more and more frustrated by the moment. Finally he stole the ball and took it to the basket at the other end. Shortly afterward, Hinkle introduced "candidate" O'Brien to Hinkle's brother-in-law. As it turned out, both O'Brien and Doyle did make the *Look* selection.

Hinkle always was sensitive to the matter of how many fans came to see his teams play, particularly in basketball. Fans responded in those immediate postwar years, but the competition for attention got tougher moving into the 1950s. Television came to the area in 1949 to begin a distraction that would grow and grow. Professional football also moved into new prominence and had its negative effect on small college programs.

In the last twenty years that Hinkle coached, crowd sizes for both football and basketball varied with the success of the team. Even student response became fickle. There was always a loyal cadre of alumni at home games, but their number became fewer during seasons with average records. So Hinkle took action to encourage attendance at his basketball games. In the mid-1950s he offered season tickets at three dollars for one, five dollars for two. The crowd quadrupled the first season and held up well into the early 1960s. Hinkle also had team success going for him then. After that crowds were inconsistent. Football became a tougher proposition. Hinkle had to concentrate on the game and not worry about crowd support. Big-school competition and other factors were too strong. Hinkle just moved ahead and coped with the disappointment he felt.

13 Football's Destiny

Football success at Great Lakes had been a joyous experience for a coach who had once faced some formidable opposition playing in the Big Ten for Chicago. Hinkle was most pleased when Butler accepted an invitation to join the Mid-American Conference, which consisted primarily of urban universities. They included Cincinnati, Western Reserve at Cleveland, Wayne State at Detroit, and Ohio University. Membership became effective with the 1946–47 basketball season. Butler shared the championship the first year and was runnerup the next two.

The Butler football program, however, did not progress as smoothly as basketball. When the school joined the new conference, it was understood it also would remain in the Indiana Conference, which would allow transfers from other schools to play immediately, as was allowed in the MAC. Just before the opener with Ball State, the transfer question was challenged by some Indiana Conference members. As a result, eight transfers (two had transferred from Indiana State, one from Ball State, both Indiana Conference members) were not allowed to play against Indiana Conference opponents. To complicate matters, freshmen, who since wartime had been allowed to play varsity at most schools, were not allowed to play in the Mid-American. That left Hinkle with a two-team mix.

When it was over, Butler was 4–0–1 against Indiana teams and 1–3 against opposition from the new conference. By then the school administration had decided to hold fast and not invest more money in the athletic program as allowed by the MAC. Butler's participation was doomed. MAC schools were off the basketball schedule by 1950–51. The phaseout was slower in football, but by 1950 Butler was in a newly formed state athletic conference, the Indiana Collegiate Conference, consisting of Evansville, Ball State, Indiana State, St. Joseph's, and Valparaiso.

At the tail end of the 1949 football season, student criticism of the football program surfaced in a *Butler Collegian* editorial. It stated that "one of three steps should be accepted: the hiring of a coach whose duties would consist of directing football only; a complete revision of the present offensive and defensive system; or the adoption of subsidization (greater financial assistance to athletes.)" One week later the Butler B-Men's Association gave Hinkle a vote of confidence. At the annual football banquet, Hinkle defended the school's policy and said "it was no way to bring a kid up" to hand him tuition and room and board without requiring a work schedule as the university did. As for his own ability to coach, he said he wanted to stay at Butler as long as Butler wanted him. It produced a standing ovation. The matter appeared to be closed for the moment.

It resurfaced thirty months later when the *Collegian* revealed that a petition with sixty-five signatures was circulating on campus demanding that Hinkle resign as football coach and the job be filled by assistant coach Boris Dimancheff. The story in the issue of May 21, 1952, stated that the move was started by members of the 1951 football team and that twenty-five of the names were those of Butler athletes. President M. O. Ross immediately came to Hinkle's defense. Whether the criticism by students eventually made the difference is speculation. Within three years, however, Butler offered athletic scholarships for the first time in its history.

In the late 1940s football was in transition and Hinkle was forced to alter his approach to the game whether some of the students thought he did or not. The substitution structure was different with the arrival of double platooning. The game was becoming more specialized and besides that the single wing was rapidly becoming a thing of the past. Passing was becoming a dominant part of the offense, built around the quarterback in the T formation. It was a radical switch but Hinkle made it.

Sylvester and twelve of his Cathedral High School teammates who went to Butler in 1946 had become familiar with the T under Dezelan. So the transition was not quite so difficult for them. Actually, three of the thirteen players from Cathedral ended up as starters. Sylvester was quarterbacking the first two years but then had to compete for his spot when Hinkle switched primarily to the newer offense by the 1948 season.

Tom Sleet went through the entire transition. He lettered at Butler in the early 1940s under the single wing, played fullback during a part of his time in military service, and went back to Butler after the war as primarily a defensive player, still put in on offense to carry the ball when short yardage was needed.

Pem Cornelius, another member of the late 1940s group, recalled how Hinkle could teach by not reacting. Cornelius missed a Labor Day practice one fall because he spent a weekend at a northern Indiana lake spot his parents owned. He overdid it and came back with an extensive sunburn. Hinkle greeted him at the next practice with "lookin' great, kid. I see ya gotta little sun. Good for you. Get those pants on and let's get going." Pem remembers a long workout followed as Cornelius suffered. Pem never let that happen again.

Then there was the responsive Hinkle. Bob Hamilton had completed his football career at Butler when he was struck down by an automobile in the fieldhouse parking lot on his way to work. Hamilton had been named the team's most valuable player. Hinkle and others staged a drive to raise money to help with nine months' hospitalization for Bob, who was married and had a small child. Once he was able to get around, Tony made him assistant freshman football coach until he guided him to a coaching job at Kokomo High School, working for another Hinkle football graduate, Clarence (Tuffy) Laymon. Hamilton ultimately became head coach there, with outstanding success.

Hinkle's football fortunes were not always that rewarding his first few years back from the navy, but he was always the same, moving steadily along from day to day, from practice to practice, from game to game. It was as if Tony knew that sooner or later things would get better—and he was right.

14 Pain and Disappointment

The Hinkle home on 46th Street was next door to the Delta Tau Delta fraternity house, and it was inevitable that some of the Delts and at times the Sigma Chis who lived across the street could be found in and around the Hinkle home. Although a few dates with the Hinkle daughters developed from this proximity, more typically it was group friendship that included impromptu snacks and sometimes lunches prepared by Jane.

Any athlete who made a move to date Barbara or Patty usually backed away when subjected to heavy kidding by team members. An athlete who was getting limited playing time would be accused of trying to get in good with the coach. Actually, Hinkle did not want to make a big deal of it, but he preferred the group friendship arrangement.

Jane had done some amateur theatricals in her younger days at Butler and had done some modeling at a major downtown department store. She impressed her next-door neighbors with her social savvy and was asked to conduct some sessions dealing with the social graces. She gave it a try, and combined with a winning personality and good humor, she did it so well that it became a required "course" at the Delt house. It stressed table manners.

But Jane didn't always score 100 percent on memory. When distracted, she had lapses. One hot summer afternoon while doing kitchen chores, she became so uncomfortable she removed her halter and went topless. Daughter Barbara was upstairs when the doorbell rang. It was a young man calling to see Barbara. Jane rushed to the door and opened it to see a startled expression come over the caller. Jane had forgotten she was topless. Barbara was embarrassed. Jane laughed about it, later.

Barbara and Patty enrolled at the university in the fall of 1949 and at the urging of their mother participated in sorority rush. Only one sorority at Butler gave them an opportunity to pledge. They turned it down. Both said years later that their mother was bothered by it more than they were. She was hurt that her own sorority was among those who passed her daughters by. As for Hinkle, the women felt that it was a matter of no great importance to him. However, he confided to a close friend at the time that of all his disappointments that was probably the worst.

The pain may have been eased a bit when Barbara was elected Miss Air Angel in a beauty contest sponsored by the student Air Reserve Officers Training Corps. She was the choice of the students in the first election involving a newly formed Independent Student Association that backed her. Barbara was also selected by a committee as one of five finalists in the traditional *Drift* Beauty Queen contest. When Hinkle learned of his daughter's recognition he was quoted as saying, "Thank god she looks like her mother."

Most nights Hinkle would get home late during this busy period of speech-making and scouting. Delt Bill Shover used to show up for dinner many a night and became sort of an adopted son and brother. Shover recalled that one night he fell asleep on the couch and everybody else went upstairs to bed. Tony came in late, didn't see his "guest," and retired too. The next morning the coach was the first one downstairs to find Shover sound asleep in his living room. Hinkle took one look at him and exclaimed: "Jesus Christ, kid, don't you ever go home?" Shover did, but he returned frequently, and he and Tony became close friends.

By spring 1950 Hinkle was back working on the baseball diamond as he had done most seasons since 1921. This time he was using a power mower and, in checking it, placed one foot in the wrong position and nearly severed it. That baseball season the coach was laid up a while, wearing a foot cast. Schwomeyer looked after the baseball team.

One of the things that 9–10 team missed was Hinkle's "fungo" hitting ability. Jimmy Doyle, who lettered all four years, said Hinkle "could drop it on a dime." This was a matter of throwing the ball up and hitting it to outfielders and infielders. But his artistry was shown when hitting to outfielders. Doyle said "he could place one that made you run and you'd miss it by one step."

Hinkle never coached at third or first. He always stayed in the dugout. His steal sign was the worst-kept secret in college baseball. He always kept score, and if he wanted a man on base to steal he'd turn the flap of the book up unless his legs were crossed. One of his players in the 1950s, Max Schumacher, who became the long-time president of the Indianapolis Indians, recalled that time and again Tony would call out to him after he got in the batter's box to "push 'em along," meaning bunt and let the runners advance. Finally Max challenged him on yelling that way because he said the catcher could hear. Hinkle's reply: "But do you think he believes me?" Discussion closed.

In basketball, 1950–51 produced the fewest wins in Tony's long coaching career. It was definitely a rebuilding year. Orvis (Shorty) Burdsall was the only starter back from the previous year, and with one exception the roster of people who earned letters was new.

15 Basketball's Lean and Plump Years

Basketball took some tumbles in the early 1950s and crowd support responded accordingly. Attendance at the Hoosier Classic had dropped severely, and Tony didn't reschedule that event for another six years. Freshman team member Keith Greve recalled how Hinkle struggled right from the beginning on deciding on a workable combination in 1951–52. He took twenty-three players to the opener at Northwestern and played all of them.

Two years later Tony decided to stir up some crowd interest. He scheduled little Rio Grande College of Ohio. It was getting a lot of national publicity because it had a player named Bevo Francis who had scored 116 points in one game. Francis, a six-foot-nine center, was scoring big totals every game on a schedule that contained little major competition. Herb Schwomeyer recalled that the upcoming match brought out what Hinkle termed the "grandstand coaches," people who attended the games at least periodically and always were eager to advise the head coach, who always patiently listened. The phones were ringing all day on the Friday before the Saturday night game. These calls were coming into the athletic office, most of them from the "coaches." They couldn't understand why Hinkle would schedule a team they claimed was led by a "clown" in scoring.

Saturday night, January 6, 1954, Bevo Francis set a new fieldhouse individual scoring record. He hit seventeen of thirty-one shots and totaled forty-eight points for the evening. The visitors won by thirteen, and nearly twelve thousand fans came to see what Bevo was all about. On Monday, Schwomeyer recalled, Hinkle looked over at him and said, "Hey, Schwo, quiet in here. Is that phone broken, you suppose?" The "coaches" were quiet.

Shortly after that basketball season ended, Hinkle learned he had been selected for a coveted honor. His name was to be added to an illustrious list of basketball greats in the Helms Athletic Foundation's College Basketball Hall of Fame. He was honored there as a coach and a player. Eventually he would also be named to the Helms Football Hall of Fame and to the prestigious Naismith Basketball Hall of Fame.

It was the beginning of many honors that would be bestowed on the coach who never looked upon himself as anyone special. A close friend, in describing Tony, called him "as common a man as I've ever met, who never was a celebrity in his own mind, who took fame and attention in stride." Another observation gives additional insight into the man, who at times made a noncaring impression. Someone called Tony "a very shy, retiring man, who was never a distant person, never above anyone . . . who could talk with you if he knew you"—but if that was not the case he had difficulty.

In the mid-1950s, Hinkle had a number of conversations with Oscar Robertson, usually considered the best player ever to come out of basketball-rich Indiana. Robertson played at Crispus Attucks, which in that era used Butler Fieldhouse almost as a home floor to handle the crowds. Robertson would drop by Butler and ask to work out. Hinkle recalled that Oscar "would work on his fundamentals for an hour before coming down to the other end of the court to play with me. I'd beat him because

I could shoot two-handed set shots and Oscar said, 'Should I learn the two-handed set?' And I said, 'No, that's old-fashioned, just keep doing what you're doing and you'll be great.' " Those visits would not be allowed under NCAA rules now, but then it was not an infraction of the rules.

Oscar and Tony became friends, and Tony wanted him to play for Butler as much as he ever wanted anybody. It was not to be. Oscar considered Butler out of respect for Hinkle, but a host of other schools were after him and he opted for the University of Cincinnati. Even a rare aggressive recruiting effort by Hinkle wasn't enough that time.

Bobby Plump got a handwritten letter from Hinkle inviting him to come up and talk about Butler. A short time later, some B-men went down to Milan to talk to him and encourage a prompt visit. That was just a few weeks after Plump's famous shot in the final seconds that gave Milan the state high school championship. Plump, who had visited Indiana University three times, Purdue twice, and Michigan State once, heard the Butler pitch after the coach emptied the dandelions he had been digging out of the outfield behind the baseball diamond. A second meeting at Butler took place a short time later. Plump said recently that it was Hinkle and what he stood for that convinced him to go to Butler. Instead of receiving a scholarship he went into the work program at the fieldhouse. A Hinkle graduate of the early 1930s took care of Bobby's room and board. That was the last year that was necessary. The next season Plump received one of the school's new athletic scholarships.

Two other incoming freshmen got full scholarships the next year. Both were headed for impressive four-year careers along with Plump. Wally Cox came out of Broad Ripple High School. He had just about convinced himself he should go play basketball at Miami of Florida when Pop Heddon contacted him. Pop was back at Butler handling the freshman teams and doing his usual recruiting job after a three-year absence setting up an athletic program at Anderson College. Pop made several visits to

Wally's home. Then came Hinkle. Wally said his parents were with him when Tony paid his visit, and he knew it was settled when Tony walked through the door. Tony and his folks hit it off immediately and Tony sat there and sipped coffee. The other talented incoming freshman was Ted Guzek from Hammond in northern Indiana. Guzek and Cox both arrived with heavy scoring credentials. It was the beginning of a scoring combination that brought national recognition back to Butler.

It didn't all come together the first season, 1954–55. Before it even started Plump was diagnosed as having a mild case of polio. He missed the early games. He said he suffered from tremendous headaches and would return to the Sigma Chi house after practice with no appetite and so tired he would just go to bed. Once Plump got back in stride he never had any further problems.

All team members were allotted basketball tickets for guests, but Hinkle would dare team members to beat him at free throws in order to receive them. Sometimes he did it blindfolded. He had been known to keep tickets if he won. If a losing player complained, he would just offer to sell them to him. Plump claimed that Hinkle never beat him at free throws but said he had never taken him on when he wanted to shoot long ones from the side. Plump said Hinkle and Dietz could both outshoot him on those. Plump was awed by Hinkle's ability to imitate the way a player moved. If he did that to a player, the player knew he was in trouble because invariably Hinkle had spotted a flaw.

As for Guzek, Hinkle was impressed with his ability to score but felt he was far too disinterested in defense. One day in practice he ordered Guzek to the other end of the floor and told him to stand there and guard the post that supported the backboard for the next few minutes. That next season Guzek led the team in scoring and was named to the Helms all-American team.

The next year, 1956–57, was a losing season, and for the only time in his career Hinkle was incapacitated most of the time. Shortly before Christmas he was stricken and the diagnosis meant that prostate surgery was necessary. Dietz took over and had to face a hot-shooting Johnny Wooden team from UCLA. The visitors hit almost 70 percent of their shots that night.

Eight nights later things got better for Dietz and the team. They came up with a two-point win over Notre Dame at South Bend, the first time that had happened since 1933. Hinkle was still in the hospital recovering from successful surgery when Dietz rushed to the hospital to see him the next day. Dietz knew that Tony was feeling better and was expecting some needling. Dietz entered Tony's room and blurted out, "It's not too tough up there if you know how to coach." The very next season Dietz was in an automobile accident and couldn't accompany Hinkle and the team for a game at Ohio State. It had been years since Butler had won at Columbus but they did this time. Hinkle couldn't wait to phone Dietz with an identical message.

The strong relationship between Hinkle and Dietz all those years Dietz was beside him had to have benefited the basketball program. Tony had complete confidence in his assistant, who sometimes suggested a substitution when Hinkle would get so absorbed in the game that he would forget such a move was appropriate. Dietz was a full-time Butler employee two years, then moved into an insurance career but continued to assist Hinkle from October until the basketball season ended. Certainly the small monetary reward was not the reason. It was just the sort of thing that happened. Hinkle wanted him there, and that was good enough for Dietz.

The early 1950s had not always produced the kinds of basketball records Hinkle usually produced. There were better days ahead, not just in basketball but in football, too.

16 Football and Fundamentals

Hinkle's approach to football was quite similar to the way he attacked the game of basketball. He was after perfection of execution. In achieving this he stressed simplicity, and in football that meant a small assortment of plays. It wasn't unusual for him to spend thirty minutes on one play and call for it over and over again. At times, players admitted, they purposely made glaring errors. When that happened, Hinkle would stop the action and have everyone walk through the play. Everybody got a rest that way.

Tony didn't place a high priority on scouting reports. Some weeks Pop Heddon and his freshmen didn't even get a a chance to scrimmage the varsity, running plays expected from the upcoming opponent. Tony preferred playing his own game, striving to get it right.

A few months after the latest burst of criticism by students and suggestions he step aside, it all started to come together again. In 1952 the team won five of eight games and tied one. The tie was the homecoming game, the kind of contest that could get a crowd's attention. Quarterback Fred Davis threw a pass that Charley Johnson caught in the end zone with ten seconds left and the receiver tied the game with the conversion.

Indiana State fans thought they were going to see their school's first-ever football win over Butler. Probably everybody there from Terre Haute agreed with Indiana State Coach Mark Dean that the ball hit the ground before Charley caught it but the officials didn't agree.

That was the last year for college football's first free-substitution rule, which had been in effect since 1941. Hinkle hadn't always fully utilized it, but when it was banned and old-style one-platoon football was brought back, he said he regretted it because the previous rule had allowed more people to play. The vote by the NCAA committee was unanimous, and the committee was headed by his old teammate Fritz Crisler. That same committee also banned the "sucker shift," which Tony had used on more than one occasion. It was a false start by the offense that could cause the defense to jump offside.

George Freyn thought he fit into Hinkle's football program pretty quickly because he had been prepared by one of Hinkle's students who operated much the same way, Frank Baird at Broad Ripple High School. Baird didn't even coach football, but he approached baseball and basketball with the same philosophy of stressing fundamentals. Freyn was switched from a guard to an end in 1953 because there was no way he was going to beat out big Bob Eichholtz. As it turned out, he made the Indiana Collegiate Conference team (he also tied for most valuable lineman honors) along with four others. The Butler team won the conference title and Hinkle was named conference coach of the year.

The return of two-way football—playing offense and defense—got Hinkle back to an old formula. He had defensive positions assigned to people strictly by what they played on offense. A Hinkle quarterback played free safety, the centers and right guards played linebacker, the left guard played nose guard, and so on. One season assistant coaches noted that the quarterback had trouble seeing the ball in the air when he had to handle punts playing safety. That was one time Hinkle had to alter his formula.

Scott Chandler was a senior on the 1955 team. His father, Dana, played on Tony's 1928–29 national championship basketball squad. By his junior year, young Chandler had "graduated" from "kid" to "Dink," Hinkle's nickname for Chandler's father. Scott said Hinkle didn't hesitate to chew anyone out when he thought it necessary but he always looked straight at the ground while doing it and invariably ended the critique with "Hey, kiddo, get in there and get the damn job done."

Despite a so-so season in 1955, the future looked brighter for Butler football. With the inauguration of athletic scholarships that season, Butler offered thirty-six of them with nearly two-thirds for football. Basketball usually got nine, and the remaining five went to other sports. Hinkle designated where they went, and he got them with the approval of an athletic committee. They covered tuition and room and board. By 1956 the football program began to show results with the help of some veterans already there. The team won six of eight games, and one loss was fumbled away by one point. The *Indianapolis Star* ran an article wondering what all those people who thought Hinkle should confine his coaching to basketball were saying now.

That season, 1956, had a strange start. Freshmen no longer were eligible to play varsity and one youngster who had received a full scholarship and was to captain the freshman team suddenly left campus after two weeks. He had enrolled at DePauw but had not withdrawn from Butler. Technically he was enrolled at both schools. James Phillippe, a Butler faculty member who was related to the youngster, accompanied Hinkle to DePauw to talk to the student. Phillippe called Hinkle's actions a lesson in the ethics Hinkle practiced. Hinkle, convinced someone had misled the student, asked one question: "Do you wish to attend Butler or DePauw?" He had told Phillippe if the answer was DePauw, they would return to Butler and consider the matter closed. The answer, however, was Butler. Hinkle then contacted DePauw's athletic director, who met with the young man. The parents also were contacted and met the same evening with all the parties concerned. The youngster, Jim Ringer, played three years on the varsity at Butler and was varsity captain his senior year. He later became a physician in Decatur, Illinois.

Sophomores were in abundance for Tony's next group (1957) led by two impressive all-city backs from Howe High School, Cliff Oilar and Kent Stewart. Stewart provided an example of how deep family loyalties can benefit a school and its athletic program. Stewart's father, Jim, had lettered for Tony in football during the early 1930s and his grandfather, class of 1880, had headed the school's Board of Trustees for many years. Hilton Brown's youngsters and most of their youngsters all had headed for Butler.

Hinkle never worked much at inspirational locker-room talks to his teams, but his style gets an A-plus from Stewart. He said that when Hinkle started talking about Butler and what it meant and what an honor it was to wear the "royal blue" for the university, "if there had been a door to tear down, I think I could have done it."

Two very personal losses for Hinkle occurred that year. Tony lost his mother. Winnie and Edgar had remained at their home on the southside of Chicago where Tony and his family had visited regularly. Edgar had remained active after retirement and at the time of his wife's death was teaching at the YMCA. Both of Tony's sisters were in the midst of teaching careers at the time. The other loss was Tony's long-time football associate, Wally Middlesworth. Wally had been a talented three-sport athlete at Butler in the early days when Hinkle was assisting Pat Page. He joined Hinkle in the 1930s and rejoined him after the war. He was Butler's first all-American, named by the Helms Foundation in basketball.

Wally would have relished what was ahead for Butler football. Over the next six seasons, the Bulldogs would lose only five games. But Hinkle was to face another major personal loss within eighteen months.

17 The Loss That Lingered

Jane and Tony's social life during their marriage was extremely limited. Tony was absorbed in his world of athletics, which included additional commitments off campus. He continued to officiate high school football games during the 1950s and always tried to accept any request to talk before high school athletic banquets. Many of those requests came from former players who were now coaches.

Social life for Jane primarily involved Butler events and annual trips to Florida with friends like the Bob Nippers that included visits to the Miami area, where the Tom Joyces had a second home. Joyce for years owned the 7-Up bottling franchise in Indianapolis. Half-a-dozen such trips were made during the summers, the only time Tony really could get away.

Seldom did one see Jane and Tony out dining together or dancing or spending an evening in Indianapolis with friends. There were times when they attended a movie together. Jane occupied herself with her daughters' lives, was involved in Red Cross activities, and served at one time as president of the Butler Women's Faculty Club. Jane also pursued numerous other interests. On vacations she enjoyed fishing, and she could be a good competitor at a bowling alley. Other interests were not enthusiastically shared by her husband. She loved music (she had studied voice and piano), she was artistic (she produced a mural of a Butler campus scene on their basement wall), and she was creative (her thank-you notes to friends were usually expressed in poetry).

Jane enjoyed social drinking, but eventually alcohol became a problem for her. In the 1950s her health began to deteriorate and by 1959 the problem had become severe. Jane died in mid-May that year at the age of fifty-two.

Although not unexpected, her death brought an extremely difficult time for Tony. Suddenly all those weekends and nights that he had devoted to putting together workable teams didn't seem so important to him. He only knew he missed his wife of nearly thirty-one years, missed her terribly. He turned to his daughters in a way he probably never had before, and they were a source of comfort to him.

Eventually Patty, whose first marriage to Fred Mason ended in divorce, moved in with her father. With her came a daughter, Kathryn, and a son, Paul (named after his grandfather). Having youngsters around the place was a welcome change, and Hinkle was pleased. Barbara and her husband, David Causey, remained in the Indianapolis area and provided some happy distractions with children Susan, Diane, Tom, and David. The daughters who once felt some distance between them and their father had grown in understanding.

Tony always had the ability to set aside his losses and turn his attention to the next win. That was the philosophy he stressed with the kids who played for him. And in these difficult personal times, the kids were easing the pain for him in the only way they knew how, by responding to his coaching and piling up wins.

18 Football Glory Years

When Hinkle's team gathered for the start of another football season in 1959, the coach worried about a lack of experience in the line. He needn't have. Only twice all season did any team score as many as two touchdowns against him. Spilling over with backfield talent and quarterback candidates, it became the first undefeated, untied team in Butler football history. Spread over two seasons, the Bulldogs only lost once.

The game the players remembered best from this era was one at Valparaiso. Butler's strong running game was effectively smothered, and late in the fourth quarter, the Bulldogs were down 7–0. A fumble set up a Butler touchdown. Hinkle disdained a two-point conversion try to take the conservative approach and kick the extra point to tie the game, 7–7. Butler held after the ensuing kickoff got the ball back and worked it to the Valpo twenty-two with seven seconds left. Hinkle had little faith in field goals and rarely if ever called for one. The legend of that Valparaiso game is that Hinkle called for a pass on the final play but the players, many of them seniors, called a timeout and rushed a kicking combination into the game. Ames Powell kicked a thirty-nine-yard field goal and Butler won, 10–7.

As far as anyone could remember, Hinkle made no mention of what happened to any player. The reason may have been expressed years later in a profile that appeared in the *Indianapolis News*. He told Dick Denny that in football he "always felt the kid out there calling plays [the quarterback] knew a helluva lot more about what was going on than you do." Hinkle always contended that on game day it should be the kids' game, a test or examination of what he and his assistants had been teaching.

The 1959 team finished in the top ten in a small-college football poll. It did not receive a bowl bid, although it was under consideration for at least one. A university policy that required equal accommodations for all players on road trips may have been a factor. Hinkle had never forgotten what happened to Tom Harding in 1938, and he was not about to let anything like that happen again. Tackle Walter Stockslager was named to the small-college all-American team. A year earlier, when the team lost only one game, guard Paul Furnish received a similar honor.

As late as 1960 Tony still valued youngsters who wanted to play more than one sport and especially someone who wanted to participate in the three he coached. Ken Freeman and Larry Shook, both of whom went on to coach in Indiana high schools, said that attitude had a definite bearing on their going to Butler. Most schools by then were wanting athletes to concentrate on one sport. But Hinkle's attitude had to be attractive to the student who was planning a career in coaching, less so to someone who thought he might make it in the professional ranks.

Hinkle launched the 1960 season with a warning, "Everyone will be out to get us," and it was undoubtedly true. Sixteen seniors were gone from teams that had compiled a twelve-game winning streak. The team extended the streak by two before St. Joseph's, an old nemesis, stopped it at Butler Bowl. It was the only loss. Butler won its third straight Indiana Collegiate Conference crown and Hinkle was named ICC coach of the year.

The most memorable game for many that year was the visit by Wabash early in the season. Some students in the dead of night burned a large W in the middle of the Bowl. There was probably nothing they could have done that would have offended Hinkle more. He spent a lot of time in the spring manicuring his baseball field, and he felt just as strongly about the appearance of his football facility. Lance Middlekauff, who was a backup quarterback, recalled the surprise that ran through the squad when the coach, who seldom launched into oration, suddenly did. It was about the "attack" on the field he dearly loved. His voice trembled. He almost sobbed. He wound it up with words like "Let's win this one for our seniors. Let's win this one for M. O. Ross [Butler President]. Let's win this one for our alumni." Middlekauff had a running gag with Tony about nicknames. Tony called him "Unitas" after Baltimore Colts quarterback Johnny Unitas, and Middlekauff called Tony "Weeb" for the highly successful coach Weeb Ewbank. When Tony finished his sentiments, Lance added softly enough that he didn't think his coach would hear, "Let's win this one for Unitas." Suddenly Hinkle was Hinkle again. He barked out, "Yes, let's win this one for Unitas because he won't be playing today." And he didn't. Quarterback Phil Long fired three long touchdown passes and had a perfect six for six that day. Butler piled up yardage on the ground and dominated, 40–7. Butler had its revenge, but the W was visible for nearly a year.

Hinkle headed into 1961 with an experienced team, and a local newspaper proclaimed that Butler wore a "can't miss label." Then on the second Saturday in September, a team of substitutes, primarily sophomores, beat the regulars in a practice game. It was probably the best thing that could have happened. Butler waltzed through another undefeated, untied season. Tommy Mont's DePauw team came the closest, 12–6. Now even the crowds were picking up on Butler football. Over eleven thousand watched the home game with Valparaiso that practically assured another conference title. It was fact one week later. Butler was now 34–2 over four years.

At the awards banquet Hinkle rated the team as one of his eight greatest but had to go on the defensive again about the program generally. The *Butler Collegian* had stated in an editorial that the team should be playing a tougher schedule and be in a stronger conference. Hinkle defended the league and reminded the school newspaper and the crowd: "We're riding a crest but someday we'll be at the bottom if history repeats itself." The biggest individual honor on that team went to senior tackle Don Benbow. His name was added to a growing list of Butler men named to the small-college all-American lineup.

All this success in football may have mellowed Hinkle a bit on spending money to feed the team. Through the years there were stories about minimal food arrangements. The menu usually consisted of two ham sandwiches and a soft drink, sometimes only an apple. But that wasn't the case after that trip to DePauw until it came time for the tip. The team was taken to a highly popular family-style restaurant near Highway 40 called Old Trails Inn. Ken Keltner, a sophomore on the team, recalled that fifty or so starving players and staff filed into the place. It took a number of waitresses to handle the crowd and all its requests. Hinkle was handed a bill of $412. He proceeded to peel off the money in five-dollar bills. Then he counted out a fifteen-dollar tip, smiled, and asked, "Is that enough?" Keltner recalled that the girl just stood there in disbelief, looking as if she might cry at any moment. Hinkle had recovered his form.

After the 1962 season, Butler's coach was quoted as saying that it was a team that "never provided a dull moment." That was true. Three games were decided by a point margin of six or less, and two ended in ties. The Bulldogs had a three-touchdown lead over Ball State and the Cardinals came back to tie with twenty-five seconds left. Guard Lee Grimm blocked a field goal attempt to salvage a tie with Wabash. St. Joseph's stopped the win streak at nineteen with a 6–0 victory in the rain and mud at Rensselaer, and a last-play safety with nine seconds left brought a win over Valparaiso, 16–14. Fans who thought the Bulldogs should be playing a tougher schedule got a jolt when the team met MAC opponent Marshall College at Huntington, West Virginia, and were outsized and outplayed.

Grimm captained the 1963 team, which won the school's sixth straight conference title. Its only defeat was at Ashland, Kentucky, to Morehead State of the Ohio Valley Conference. The game most fans remembered, though, was with Ball State at the Bowl. Officials ruled that a punt by Ball State was dead when touched and could not be run in for a touchdown. Butler did just that and the touchdown was called back. Hinkle argued the rule and wouldn't give up. In a rare moment in Hinkle's history, he was ordered off the field. At halftime, Jim Hauss produced a rule book and showed it to the officials. They agreed they had made the call incorrectly. When they returned for the second half, they ran into Hinkle and the chief official apologized. Hinkle's response: "Oh, fellas, I was just tryin' to help you." Butler won anyway by two touchdowns.

Frustration awards that season would have been fitting for two other conference opponents, DePauw and Indiana State. A newspaper account said that "the host Tigers chewed up Butler every place but on the scoreboard." Each team scored two touchdowns, but DePauw failed twice in attempts for two-point conversions. At Terre Haute the Sycamores won all the statistics but Butler won the game, 7–6. Ron Captain intercepted two key passes and knocked an ISU runner out of bounds as he went for two points on the conversion try after Indiana State's touchdown. That happened late in the final quarter.

That was the only time Tony had a relative playing for him. Earning his letter in both 1962 and 1963 was Jack Lord, who played on the line. His mother was Tony's sister Florence, and she and her husband looked at Butler football with a new personal interest.

When the 1963 season ended, Grimm had been named to the small-college all-American team and Hinkle once again was the ICC coach of the year. It had been a glorious era, but as the coach had remarked seven years earlier, "riding a crest" isn't permanent. As usual, he was right.

19 Basketball's Tourney Times

It was bound to happen sooner or later. It did in 1958. A Butler basketball team was going to a national collegiate postseason tournament. It was one of twelve teams selected to compete for the National Invitational title at Madison Square Garden.

This four-year process began to develop when three talented scorers enrolled and were moved into varsity action their first year. Only polio, as previously mentioned, delayed Plump's participation at the very beginning with Guzek and Cox. But while there were moments of championship-style play, these teams had losing seasons two of the first three years.

In 1957 Greve came back from military service to add his scoring skills to the trio. Sophomore Ken Pennington moved up from the freshman program (freshmen no longer played varsity basketball) to handle center, and Bill Scott from the great Crispus Attucks program moved in to become an outstanding sixth man.

At the season-end banquet for 1957–58, Hinkle made this observation about the best shooting team he ever coached (sixth in the nation in field goal accuracy and fourth in free throws):

"They shot well because they had to. If they passed the ball, they probably felt they wouldn't get it back."

Cox and Plump never stopped exchanging barbs about that. Cox claimed that if Bobby hadn't always maneuvered him into taking the ball out so much, Cox too would have broken some scoring records their senior year. But it was Plump who broke O'Brien's career record, followed by Greve and Guzek, who also topped it. In addition, Plump established a new Butler individual scoring record with forty-one points (including seventeen of seventeen free throws) against usually difficult Evansville at the fieldhouse.

Hinkle had something else to say about that team at season end. It was typical, subtle, tongue-in-cheek Tony: "They mostly coached themselves. Why, in the huddle I couldn't get a word in edgewise. They'd talk like a bunch of old women." Actually Hinkle had things under control. The long fundamental drills and the emphasis on defense (as Guzek could testify) were still in evidence.

One of the many signals that this team was something special came at the revived Hoosier Classic. On opening night Butler, utilizing a well-balanced scoring attack, defeated Indiana University. McCracken had shared the Big Ten championship the previous season and would be the sole champion that season.

As for that season's visit to the Garden, one newspaper account described the team as one that was "wound as tight as an eight-day clock." One of the best free-throw-shooting teams in the nation missed thirteen of them that night. It matched St. John's of New York in field goal accuracy but lost by seven points. Pennington, who was six feet five and weighed 210 pounds, had a problem that night. He had developed a beautiful fake under the basket that faked out the officials as well as the opposition. The officials were convinced he was dragging his pivot foot and issued some crucial travel calls. Plump was named to the West's college all-star team.

Despite the departure of all four of his high-scoring starters,

Hinkle sensed he had another winner ahead for the next year, 1958–59. He was quoted as saying, "We're going to be better than a lot of people think right now." Built around Pennington and Scott, the Butler team went 0–5 at the beginning and Hinkle's optimism seemed misplaced. But the team was developing. It beat the defending Ivy League champion, Dartmouth, in overtime and followed that with an upset of fifth-ranked Tennessee. Hinkle guided his team to another Classic win over I.U. and a home win over Notre Dame. It took three overtimes to stop the Irish at the fieldhouse. Butler finished the season 18–8. Two of the late losses were on the road to ICC teams.

The bulk of the season scoring came from Pennington and Scott. The team wasn't quite as accurate as its predecessor but it won more games. It was extremely adept at defense. This also was the team that brought Tony's four hundredth Butler victory. It occurred at the fieldhouse on a Saturday night, February 7, a ten-point win over Ball State. That game was followed by a ceremony marking the moment. Hinkle described this squad as "a bunch of average kids who fought and dug and scratched."

It earned a return to the NIT and the Garden. The first few hours of the trip were disconcerting. Weather delayed the plane's departure, and both the team and the coaches appeared tired and down when they reached New York City two and a half hours behind schedule.

Butler's first-round opponent was Fordham, favored by twelve points in the eyes of the experts. The bigger Rams had a tie on their hands five minutes into the second half. Pennington, Scott, and John Jones then scored twenty-seven of the next forty Butler points and Butler won by fourteen. Newspaper reports said "alert ball hawking" was the difference.

Hinkle's next assignment was top-seeded Bradley two evenings later. Butler put on a strong rally late in the game but came up short and Bradley won by six. Again Butler had Garden free-throw trouble, hitting only half of their free throws. The rags-to-riches season was over.

Coach John Wooden and his UCLA Bruins came calling the next season, 1959–60. Wooden had played at the Butler Fieldhouse as a member of the Martinsville High School team within days after it had opened. The Martinsville team had gone to the final game of the state tournament and lost by one point. Around that time Tony had talked to Wooden about enrolling at Butler. Wooden had opted for Purdue for a number of reasons but had always respected Tony and the way he operated. A few years later, when Wooden was coaching at South Bend Central High School, he was in the crowd at Notre Dame to watch Butler and the Irish tangle in basketball. It was in midwinter and snow had prevented one of the referees from getting there. Hinkle and Notre Dame coach Keogan spotted Wooden and he was asked to meet with them. They told him he was the only one they could agree on to fill in for the missing referee. Wooden wasn't enthusiastic. He hadn't refereed much. Finally, he issued a warning. He said he would do it, but if either coach complained over a call he would leave the floor. Wooden had no trouble. At Butler Fieldhouse that midwinter night in 1959, Wooden did have some trouble, though. Butler shot 57 percent and Pennington led the scoring. Wooden's taller team lost to Hinkle by six points.

By this season the basketball was the bright color that is common today. For years the color had varied but had tended to be a muddy brown. Hinkle wanted to standardize it and brighten it so it would stand out better for the large crowds that were now common. The Spaulding Company worked on perfecting a ball that met the requirements Hinkle wanted. Tests were run at an NCAA tourney final in Louisville in the late 1950s. Teams used the brighter products in practice. The NCAA was favorably impressed and the color was promptly adopted.

The most amazing game that season (1959–60) was at Crawfordsville, where Butler and Wabash literally played a game and a half. It went five overtimes before the home team prevailed.

Twice that winning season Hinkle's team met Ohio State,

which carried a roster that included John Havlichek, Jerry Lucas, and a fellow who would eventually take up residence in Indiana, Bob Knight. Ohio State won handily both evenings but Knight's offensive contribution was modest. He scored four points one night, two the other. Knight recalled that his coach, Fred Taylor, had great respect for Hinkle's coaching abilities and used what he called a "Butler defense." It was geared to do particular things to deal with a Butler-type offense. Knight said that term was used throughout the three seasons he played for Taylor.

Indiana University's first Knight team played at Butler after Hinkle had retired from coaching. George Theofanis was the coach then, and Hinkle was working with Tom Carnegie on the play-by-play televised report of the game. With two or three minutes left, I.U. led by a big enough margin that Knight called a timeout and told his team to spread out and use up time and not to go for points. Moments later Joby Wright shot and scored. Knight called another timeout and repeated his message. Wright again shot and scored. Knight watched the delayed broadcast later at his home. At the first timeout he heard Hinkle tell Carnegie that from what he knew about this kid (Knight) there would be no more shots taken. After Wright fired, Knight heard Tony say he must have been given some bad information on this new coach because he just didn't think they would play it that way. Tony said he was sure there would be no more shots after the second timeout. After the second shot, Tony said that "whoever told me how this kid was going to coach didn't know what he was talking about." By that time Knight was yelling at his TV set, "Damn it, Tony, I'm trying to keep these kids from shooting." I.U. won by eleven points.

Even by the late 1950s Hinkle was still finding youngsters who reacted to the fieldhouse mystique. Dick Haslam was a member of the Crawfordsville High School team that lost out to Fort Wayne South in the 1958 state tourney final game played at the fieldhouse. Haslam called it a beautiful place to play the game. He said there was just a certain sound heard when the ball rebounded or hit the floor.

The athletic scholarship program that had been established at Butler had helped encourage athletes to consider Butler, but more and more it took recruiting to get the job done. The budget was practically zero, and Pop Heddon could accomplish only so much for his busy boss, who didn't believe in an aggressive approach. Still the allure of playing for Hinkle constituted an effective recruiting tool. Time after time coaches encouraged top talent to consider Butler because of Hinkle. It also was a fact that any Hinkle graduate who planned to head into coaching could count on prompt job consideration in Indiana and surrounding states.

More direct recruiting was going on for Butler. A number of alumni were out looking and a few made preliminary contacts with athletes. One of the more active alumni in this regard for a number of years was Robert Parr, who became university physician in the mid-1950s. Parr said he and the others found plenty of fellow alumni whom he described as members of the "Hinkle admiration society." Parr would send out the word and someone would plant the seed. Hinkle really had no part in it except to insist that everybody know the NCAA rules and abide by them.

A special brochure was prepared by the university that stressed the academic aspect of being an athlete at Butler. Parents learned that classes came first and that practice sessions came second if there was ever a schedule or deadline conflict. The brochure also explained that road games were arranged for minimal intrusion and that coaches in no way exerted influence on a faculty member who had an athlete in class. From time to time a member of the faculty accompanied the party making a call on the parents of a prospect.

It is quite likely that Jeff Blue, who played a key role in getting the Butler basketball team into the NCAA tourney, would never have come to Butler if it had not been for this extra

In the 1930s Hinkle was firmly established on the American athletic scene and was a member of the national collegiate basketball rules committee. (Photo courtesy Indianapolis Newspapers, Inc.)

Bob Dietz (31) and Jerry Steiner (30) were teammates on Hinkle basketball squads in the late 1930s. Both were effective two-handed set shot scorers. Dietz became Hinkle's long-time assistant in basketball. Steiner was one of Hinkle's first standout little men—the type for which Hinkle became noted.

Tony, Jane, and daughters Barbara and Patricia always lived within walking distance of the Butler athletic facilities. This photo was taken during the 1930s when the girls still thought it was fun to pick up debris at the fieldhouse on Sundays.

Jane Hinkle modeled clothes for a downtown Indianapolis department store. On this occasion daughter Patricia shared the limelight with her.

Tom Harding was one of the first of many black athletes to star for Hinkle. He excelled not only in football but also baseball and track.

Hinkle was commissioned an officer in the U.S. Navy following the 1941–42 basketball season. He coached football and basketball for two seasons at the Great Lakes Naval Training Center. When World War II ended he was stationed on Guam.

When Butler's coach returned to campus, a special welcome home ceremony was held in his honor. On the platform are (from left) student Howard Sharfin, Hinkle, Bob Nipper, Frank Heddon, Wally Middlesworth, and Hilton U. Brown, president of the Butler Board of Trustees.

Like most coaches in the first postwar months, Hinkle was besieged by ex-GI athletes. The surprise in basketball was little Ralph (Buckshot) O'Brien, fresh out of Indianapolis's Washington High School. A starter four years, he set several individual scoring records.

Sports broadcaster Tom Carnegie and Coach Hinkle struck up a friendship when Tony appeared on Carnegie's sportscasts on WIRE radio in the late 1940s. Later they worked telecasts for years on Channel Six covering state high school basketball tournament games.

This was a familiar Hinkle look after a football game. Hinkle always reviewed his strategy and never hesitated to blame himself if it didn't work.

Hinkle was a master at fungo hitting during baseball workouts. It was said that he could hit the ball to any spot he wanted, challenging the outfielders especially. He also pitched batting practice and was adept at forcing batters to hit to wherever he desired.

Coach Hinkle's first undefeated, untied football season came in 1959. He never enjoyed being carried aloft, even at a time like this, but he wasn't about to discourage it, either. Two years later it happened again. (Photo courtesy Indianapolis Newspapers, Inc.)

Nowhere was Hinkle's great faith in his assistants more evident than with Bob Dietz. It was Dietz who worked with the basketball team each year until football season ended, and Dietz determined most of the basketball rosters, knowing who would fit into the Hinkle system. Dietz assisted Hinkle from 1946 to 1970.

Little Bob Plump (left), who as a high school player hit a shot in the last seconds that gave Milan the state title, was a senior at Butler in 1957–58 when Hinkle took his basketball team to his first postseason tournament. Plump, Keith Greve, and Ted Guzek all broke Buckshot O'Brien's career scoring record that season.

Butler's 1958–59 basketball team, with several new faces, surprised a lot of people. It brought Hinkle his four hundredth win and advanced to the second round of the NIT.

Not until Hinkle was in his final years of football coaching did an Indiana State University team beat Butler. This photo was taken at halftime of a game in 1966 that Butler went on to win—the twenty-first and last time Hinkle beat them. (Photo by Frank Fisse; courtesy Indianapolis Newspapers, Inc.)

Hinkle had a paternal attitude toward his playing fields. When Wabash students burned a W on his football field, he wept. This photo was taken later, during a high school band day at Butler Bowl.

Assistant coaches at Butler almost always were Hinkle graduates. Hinkle is shown here with three of them (from left): Frank Heddon, Bill Sylvester (who succeeded Hinkle as head football coach), and Jim Hauss.

It wasn't a winning season, but the 1965–66 basketball squad did give Tony his five hundreth win. Lon Showley (left), Gene Milner, and Bill Brown (30) escort the coach off the floor after the win over Indiana State.

Hinkle's last basketball team featured not one but two little men who scored heavily and contributed to a winning season in 1969–70. Billy Shepherd (14) led the scoring, while Steve Norris (10) was one of the most accurate shooters from the field in Butler history.

Veteran sports writers gather around Tony Hinkle shortly before the ceremony marking his retirement. They include Bob Collins of the *Indianapolis Star* (lower right) and Corky Lamm (right) and Wayne Fuson (immediate left), both of the *Indianapolis News.*

The capacity crowd was up on its feet more than once the night Tony Hinkle coached his final basketball game. Hinkle looked ill at ease until he stepped to the microphone and told the crowd his main interest that night was in seeing a good basketball game. He did.

Until 1988 Hinkle played golf regularly with old friends. Bill Davis (right) clears the way as Tony prepares to swing. With them are Tom Warner (left of Hinkle), who succeeded Hinkle as Butler's athletic director, and Bob Nipper. (Photo courtesy Indianapolis Newspapers, Inc.)

In 1989 the old coach, who was still getting to his office in the fieldhouse every day, posed with basketball coach Barry Collier. It coincided with the announcement that Butler's fieldhouse—renamed Hinkle Fieldhouse to honor Tony in 1965—would undergo a major renovation.

Historic Hinkle Fieldhouse got a new lease on life, with the first renovation phase completed in time for the 1989–90 season. Many of the bleachers were replaced by new chairback seats, and one of them invariably was occupied by the man who arrived on campus seven years before the place opened.

volunteer effort. Jeff and his older brother, Mike, were close, and what happened to Mike was important to Jeff. Both played on the Bainbridge High School basketball team in the Greencastle area, but Mike didn't get the playing time Jeff did. Butler offered Mike a scholarship and a chance to play basketball. No other school did that.

Jeff was a senior in high school when his brother played freshman basketball for Heddon. He frequently visited the campus and began to feel comfortable about the place. When recruiting time rolled around, over ninety schools went after Jeff, some with what Jeff called "outlandish" incentives. His father had studied the rules and whenever he felt someone was stretching them, he lost interest. In the midst of all this, Blue said, Hinkle phoned him and said he wanted to talk. Jeff assumed the coach would come over to see him like most of the others. He found Hinkle hadn't even thought of that. He expected Blue to come see him. Blue said his first thought was "I think I like this guy's style."

Blue's interview took place on the lower level of the fieldhouse in the equipment room. He sat on the edge of an old wooden desk and Tony sat in an old rocking chair. The conversation lasted about ten minutes. Blue said Hinkle told him he thought he'd like it at Butler, that he'd fit into "our brand of basketball," that no effort was made to create a star, and that a scholarship included tuition, books, room and board, and nothing more. Blue thought, "Gosh, it's a good thing I want to go here." Just as he was leaving came this comment from Hinkle: "Now if you decide you don't want this scholarship we're offering, you be sure and let me know because we don't want to cheat some other kid out of it."

Tony had only three lettermen back for 1960–61, so it was going to be another building year while Jeff Blue played freshman ball. A starting team of all sophomores and juniors beat Wisconsin and Michigan and scared second-ranked Bradley, 71–65. Little sophomore Gerry Williams (five feet eight) surfaced that night with twenty-seven points, teaming with Tom Bowman, who had nineteen. The team visited Wooden's eleventh-ranked Bruins but couldn't get closer than ten points.

I.U. had withdrawn from the Hoosier Classic (some Butlerites said it was because McCracken hated to lose to Butler), so Illinois was invited. Only 6,100 fans showed up to see Butler beat the Illini when center Don Wilson scored twenty-three points. Butler then came back the next night and beat Purdue on a Williams jump shot with nine seconds left. It was a night when Purdue all-American Terry Dischinger scored thirty-four points and broke a bunch of Classic records. It also marked the end of the Classic series. Once again Indiana State and Evansville beat Butler on their home courts, but that didn't keep Hinkle's team from winning another ICC crown.

Success came as no surprise in 1961–62. Hinkle had all his starters back along with Blue. Blue made a difference in more ways than one. He and Hinkle had some colorful confrontations early in the season.

The season had hardly started when Blue informed his coach that he had received a notice to report for a military physical. Apparently his deferment papers weren't in the right hands. Hinkle didn't consider it critical until he realized that the physical was scheduled just a few hours before Butler was to host Michigan at the fieldhouse. Hinkle made a phone call and got it straightened out. As it turned out, Butler beat Michigan that night.

At practice the following week, nothing was going right. Mistakes were erupting thick and fast. Blue said that at one point he turned to drive toward the basket when he bounced the ball off his foot and out of bounds. Hinkle, who was sitting on a basketball at the edge of the floor, threw his hands in the air, lost his balance, and fell off the floor onto the concrete. Everything went stone silent except for Blue, who burst out laughing and couldn't quit. Hinkle approached, his scowl set, to within ten feet of Blue, then said, "Blue, I should have let the military have you."

In some of the games the talented center had free-throw trouble. It happened at Peoria, Illinois, that season when Butler was threatening to upset Bradley, a team that had won the last seventy-one games at home. Williams and Bowman couldn't miss that night, with thirty and twenty-five points respectively. Butler was barely ahead with about sixteen seconds left, Blue recalled. Hinkle called time to talk strategy, certain Bradley would foul to get the ball. He also said, "We all know who they will foul." Hinkle then looked at Jeff: "Blue, if you get the ball, get rid of it. Don't let them touch you. If you don't have the ball and they try to touch you, run. If you have to run across the floor and out the door into the snow, don't let them touch you." Butler won.

The Bulldogs got another double win over Notre Dame that season. At South Bend Williams and Blue each got twenty-six points. It was a warm night for Butler even though it was nine degrees below zero outside. Hinkle guided his team to another ICC crown, even beating Indiana State and Evansville on their home courts. A lone conference defeat came at Valparaiso.

For the third time in five seasons Hinkle had his team in a postseason tourney, this time—for the first time—in the twenty-five team NCAA event. It started for Butler at the Memorial Coliseum in Lexington, the home of Adolph Rupp's powerful Kentucky Wildcats. The opening opponent was Bowling Green, which had ended the regular season ranked eighth in the nation. The team's game revolved around six-ten center Nate Thurmond. The Falcons threw up a tight zone defense to contain Blue, but Bowman and Williams provided accuracy from outside. Butler trailed most of the game, then went ahead on two free throws in the final seconds. Butler got the ball back, threw it away, then prevented Thurmond and his group from scoring in the last sixteen seconds. Butler won by one point.

Then it had to face Kentucky, ranked third in the country. The game was played at Iowa City four days later. Newspaper accounts said the team "scrapped and scrambled" (Williams got twenty and Blue nineteen), but Kentucky won by twenty-one points.

Butler got to play one more game that season. It was a consolation game with Western Kentucky the next night. Butler caught fire after a lethargic first half and hit over 50 percent of its shots to send the game into overtime. That's when the Bulldogs really scored, with 64 percent accuracy and a one-point victory.

A lot of Butler fans enjoyed that season but no one more than the fellow who first learned about the game in a public park on the southside of Chicago. It was his thirty-third Butler basketball team, and its 22–6 record was his best.

20 The Late Seasons

Dick Dullaghan never forgot the day he and Art Beck were in their defensive positions, a three-deep zone, and "a guy comes runnin' down the middle between us. They hit him with a perfect pass and he scores a touchdown." Both Dullaghan and Beck were veteran football players at Butler who weren't supposed to let things like that happen. They ran off the field, looking sheepishly at each other and wondering who would get the blame. Hinkle, looking at both of them in disbelief, yelled out, "What are you guys doin'?" Both had been ruled guilty. Fortunately Butler was way ahead and it didn't seriously affect the final score.

Dullaghan recalled his embarrassment: "We knew that we'd blown it and we knew our coach would not let it pass by without definite comment but without ranting and raving and that later he would needle us just to remind us he hadn't forgotten." Dullaghan said that was the kind of thing you learned from Hinkle. He could pick a player apart when he needed it and laugh with him when he needed that, too.

The Dullaghan-Beck gaffe came in 1964 when rule changes had opened up the return of double platooning, playing defensive and offensive units. There were some restrictions, however, and Hinkle still was using players for both sides of the game. Both quarterback Beck and halfback Dullaghan received the top team awards when the season ended.

The season was one of rebuilding and no one expected much. The team lost four games (two in the conference), tied another, and still ended in a four-way tie for the ICC crown.

The next year the team won five of eight with Joe Purichia at quarterback. Hinkle still was giving his quarterbacks a lot of freedom to call their own plays. But there were exceptions. During one game Tony sent a pass play in to Purichia, written on a piece of paper. At the end it said: "Tell the guys and get rid of it." Purichia considered chewing it up, then stuck it in his helmet. The play didn't work. Purichia blamed himself for missing the open man. After the game the note dropped out of his helmet just as Hinkle walked by. Quietly Hinkle said, "That's okay, kid." Purichia never forgot the sympathetic tone of the comment.

No one who was in Butler Bowl when the season closed that year (1965) will ever forget the last ten minutes of the game with Western Kentucky. Butler trailed, 20–0. Purichia, Dullaghan, and center Joe Dezelan, Jr., all were playing their last game for Hinkle. After three quarters of what newspaper accounts called "inept blocking and tackling," team members came to life. The Bulldogs scored three touchdowns and with ninety seconds left missed a conversion to leave it tied. One minute later a pass interception led to the win. It was Hinkle's last winning football season at Butler.

Inconsistency marked the next football season, 1966. Butler beat a strong Evansville team, but three-point losses to Ball State and Valparaiso left the school second in the ICC, and every time the team ventured outside the state, it lost. That also was the year the ICC's future began to look questionable. DePauw was planning to withdraw. An era was about to end in more ways than one.

The next season it finally happened. Indiana State, a school that was heading into a stronger commitment to athletics and enrollment, beat a Hinkle team. Twenty-six times the two schools had met (all but two of those meetings involved Hinkle) without a Sycamore victory, though there had been some close ones as well as controversial games. Butler only won the fumble count, but quarterback Ed Bopp said the Sycamores didn't cause many of them.

Bopp noted that this was only the second football game ever played in Indiana on artificial turf. Indiana State was one of the first colleges to install it. One week earlier the Sycamores had played their first game on it. Bopp said the surface didn't work very well, particularly with the old shoes that he and others were wearing. At any rate, Butler fumbled six times that day and the hosts had an historic win, 23–7.

When Butler went to Muncie, it got embarrassing. The Ball State Cardinals romped at will and won, 65–7. When the season ended both Ball State and Indiana State announced their withdrawal from the conference. Times had changed, and both schools were moving into a different level of competition.

Hinkle was not the kind to let other schools' commitments change his outlook. When Butler lost its first three games in 1968, he was quoted in the *Indianapolis Star* as saying he thought Butler's future showed promise, and he saw improvements when his team lost another one to Indiana State. One week later his team dominated St. Joseph's. The media responded that Hinkle was "up to his old trick of winning," but there was only one more win that season.

Until the late 1960s the athletic scholarship funds did not keep up with tuition increases. Rising costs were diminishing their value year by year. That was changed in 1968. Still, the recruitment budget was unrealistic. In 1969, after Don Benbow joined the football staff as assistant coach, he made one recruiting trip and found he used all the allocated funds, $250.

Still, Hinkle magic kept the less-expensive basketball program going. The school continued to schedule top teams, particularly in December before conference schedules began. More people than ever before watched Butler basketball in 1962–63. NCAA fever hadn't cooled. Over eleven thousand saw Butler stop old rival Evansville's bid for an undefeated conference season. Butler's win stopped a seventeen-game winning streak the Aces hoped to take into the small-college NCAA postseason tourney. For the season, crowds at the fieldhouse approached 120,000. The biggest crowd, just under thirteen thousand, came to see Ohio State. The Bucks, who were to be Big Ten champions, won but it was close.

The 1962–63 team managed to knock off a few giants. At Ann Arbor, Gerry Williams stole the ball with seconds left, scored, and got fouled for a three-point play. Then with four seconds left his shot was allowed on a goal-tending call and Hinkle's kids had a one-point win. They also got another one over Notre Dame in the fieldhouse as Blue led the scoring. Tom Bowman broke the three-year scoring record that season.

Blue recalled that Hinkle was pretty proud of his teams of that era, though he would never let team members know directly. Blue said Hinkle was quoted as telling one prospective student that "we've got Bowman from Martinsville, who's a fine shooter from out, Williams, who is a terrific high jumper and point guard, and this 'kangaroo' from Bainbridge."

The "kangaroo" was back for one more season (1963–64), and when it ended he had broken Bowman's scoring record and was named most valuable player. It was not one of Hinkle's better seasons. But little five-nine guard Larry Shade was definitely a crowd pleaser. He did an effective job hawking all-Big Ten guard Mel Garland, which contributed to a win over Purdue, and he led the Butler scoring (twenty-two points) the night they played Wooden's Bruins at the Los Angeles Coliseum. That team was the first of John's ten national champions.

The 1964–65 season was a losing one, but it brought some surprises too. Ohio State won in the last eighteen seconds at

Columbus by just one point. Dave Sanders had thirty points that night. The team produced a happy sixty-fifth birthday for Tony with a one-point win over Michigan State. It also upset Bradley, though only fifteen hundred fans showed up at the fieldhouse to see it.

By the time the next season (1965–66) rolled around Tony had been inducted into the Naismith Basketball Hall of Fame and had had the fieldhouse named for him. This honor came after forty-five years of service to Butler. It came straight from the Board of Trustees and Tony was pleasantly surprised: "Naturally, I'm very happy they think I've done something to warrant such an honor. . . . I'll try to live up to what the trustees think of me."

Larry Shade had a lot to do with success in 1965–66. As Tony said, "I think Larry belongs in our miracle corner of little guys." The *Drift* explained why: "Maintaining a starting position for three years, the guard from Seymour, Indiana, was the sparkplug of the team. Larry was everywhere on the floor, guarding, shooting, and rebounding. He outplayed some of the biggest names in collegiate basketball."

Of course, Shade wasn't the only one. The Butler team also depended on big Ed Schilling, who had transferred from the University of Cincinnati and was now eligible to play. Schilling came into his own the night the team gave Tony his five hundredth Butler win at Hinkle Fieldhouse. Ed got forty-two points, and a newspaper account said his "sticky, saggin' defense" kept the ball away from Indiana State's two best scorers. More than seven thousand saw Butler come from behind in the second half. It was on the eve of Tony's sixty-sixth birthday and a large cake was provided. That team went on to win sixteen games, including one over a taller Michigan club that had all-American Cazzie Russell and was ranked third in the nation at the time. The team even outrebounded the Wolverines, and one knowledgeable observer said that "every Butler player on the floor was a hero."

There had been an adjustment period for Schilling. As he recalled, it took him a while to appreciate the off-the-court side of the Hinkle system: "When I got to Cincinnati they met me and took my bags up to my room and took my dad to the football game. When I arrived at Butler there was no one there to meet me so the next day I went to Coach Hinkle's office and said, 'Well, I'm here,' and he said 'Good, glad to have you.' " A short time later Schilling found himself on a Butler Bowl cleanup crew, part of the terms of his scholarship. Schilling said he really began to get his values straight at Butler, where the administration "didn't adulate athletes." He had two productive seasons, though his last one (1966–67) was the first of three losing seasons for Tony, something that had never happened before.

Hinkle teams rarely lost control to mix it up out on the floor, but it happened the next season (1967–68) in a December holiday game with Purdue. Gary Cox and Bill Mauck (with a broken nose) and one Boilermaker were tossed out of the game. Otherwise Butler had it together that day with thirteen thousand at the fieldhouse to watch. Sophomore Rick Mount scored twenty-three points, but John Nell kept after him and he missed seventeen times from the field. Purdue, outrebounded and up against a team that shot over 50 percent, lost by seventeen. But that game was the exception and not the rule that season.

Early in January the man who had played such a strong role in guiding his son toward certain values and standards in life died in a nursing home in Chicago. Edgar Hinkle was ninety-two at the time of his death. His long life had enabled him to see Paul achieve not only success but also national respect as a teacher and coach. He could be very proud of his son.

Tony made a most beneficial decision earlier that school year. He went to Carmel High School at the request of one of his players from the post–World War II era. Bill Shepherd was athletic director at Carmel, and he wanted Tony to serve as an official at one of his school's home football games. Hinkle had eased up on such commitments in the 1960s, but when one of his kids asked he tried to accommodate.

Some time during the evening (probably before the game started) Shepherd took his son, Billy, to the locker room to talk to his old coach. Billy was having a high-scoring career at Carmel, preparing for his last year there. After the conversational preliminaries were over, Billy recalled, Hinkle asked him what size shoe he wore. When Billy answered size nine, Hinkle said, "That's good because we have plenty of shoes down at Butler in that size." Some other schools talked with Billy but when it got right down to it the old "fieldhouse mystique" and Hinkle's identity and reputation still had an impact, particularly when the player's father had gone through the program and could describe it so well. Billy enrolled at Butler.

Forty-five hundred fans showed up at Hinkle Fieldhouse for the freshman-varsity basketball game held one week before the 1968–69 season opened. If they came to get a glimpse of just how good the highly publicized Billy was, they weren't disappointed. His two free throws with seven seconds left gave the "young upstarts" a 74–72 win over the varsity. Billy totaled twenty-five for the evening.

Early-season wins weren't easy to come by that year, but one night in mid-December Tony left his starting five in the whole game to beat stubborn Western Kentucky by two points. Scott Neat (who later became Butler's baseball coach) was at one guard and Steve Norris the other. Clarence Harper was the center, Garry Hoyt and Bob Schroeder the forwards. Twelve days later, using just seven men, Tony's team beat a tall New Mexico team in overtime. A not uncommon happening at Butler through the Hinkle years occurred at the semester break. Harper lost out on grades and Dave Bennett emerged as an effective replacement the rest of the season. Seal also contributed that season but losses again outnumbered wins.

When Hinkle's thirty-eighth baseball team completed its schedule with a highly successful 12–5 season, it was pretty clear that Tony was facing just one more cycle of seasons. Retirement time was approaching. Hinkle was not the kind of person to stew about such matters. He would simply turn his attention to the next thing, football, just as he had all those seasons before.

21 Last Teams and Farewell

It became official early in September when the university announced that Tony Hinkle would retire after the school year was completed, actually effective August 1. One of the first to react was John Wooden: "College athletics will have lost just a tremendous person. No, not just as a coach. He is tremendous there, too, but so much more. Tony is a great, warm person and always has been. I'll always feel just the association with him has helped me."

One week later Hinkle appeared jolted by what happened at his team's football opener in Butler Bowl. Akron rolled up fifty-two points and Butler failed to score. One newspaper reported that Hinkle feared "we are weaker." The previous season the team had won only twice. At any rate, one week later Butler turned on Indiana Central, 57–0. But that was an exception. Defeats came from Ball State and Wabash on the road; the second win came at home over DePauw between those two games.

A bright spot in this final year for Hinkle was the passing ability of his quarterback, Dick Reed. Dick and his twin brother, Dave, had come out of Catlin High School in east-central Illinois. Both wanted to play football and basketball, and schools recruiting them wanted them to stick to one sport. Their coach talked to them about Hinkle, and they ended up at Butler on athletic scholarships. Both were serious students; when class demands interfered, they backed away from basketball. Dick had proved himself by 1968 and took over quarterbacking chores. An effective passer, he set a new yardage record in 1969.

Dick Reed recalled that Hinkle's last football season was the sport's one hundredth year of existence and everybody's football helmet carried the number 100 on it. One day Tony called out, "Hey, 100, come over here," and everybody looked up at the same time. Reed said that the coach called him by name on the last day of practice that season and "I didn't know how to handle it."

Reed broke the school passing record in a game at St. Joseph's but the home team won by three points, scoring a touchdown in the final minute. After two more losses, to Indiana State and Evansville, the team played the last game at home against Valparaiso. The Crusaders were going for the conference title, with the conference now minus Ball State and Indiana State and with DePauw in its last year.

Something happened that day. Butler was a different team. In all probability it was an emotional response for their coach, but it wasn't because Tony demanded it. That wasn't the Hinkle way. Reed recalled what Hinkle told his players just before they left the locker room: "Coach Hinkle told us don't win this game for me. Win it for yourselves. But everybody was emotional. Everybody wanted Tony to go out on a winning note." Reed hit twenty-six of thirty-nine passes for 276 yards and two touchdowns. Mike Caito scored eight points on five conversions and one field goal. Jim Wallace caught eight of the passes. Randy Beldon gained fifty-seven yards in eleven carries. At one point Reed lured the whole Valparaiso team into chasing him, then spun and threw the ball to a wide-open Arnold Kirschner for a touchdown. It was much like that Great Lakes play Tony got twenty-six years earlier when he beat Notre Dame. When the final football day was over, underdog Butler had won 38–20. The Bulldogs carried Tony off the field.

Tony's successor was Bill Sylvester, who had returned to be with his old coach in 1964 as assistant in football and unofficial assistant athletic director.

Tony Hinkle's last Butler basketball team (1969–70) was a contrast of extremes. It scored more and allowed more baskets than any team in Butler history. It averaged eighty-nine points per game while giving up eighty-eight points. Tony described his squad this way: "Their game was run and shoot and it took me a while to learn that. I tried to slow 'em down at first . . . and I found out when you slow these guys down, they stop."

It was also a team that excelled in accuracy. From the field the team shot 49.5 percent and from the free throw line an impressive 72 percent. A big contributor was five-foot-eight senior guard Steve Norris, the team's second leading scorer, who hit 55 percent of his shots and almost all of his free throws, 89.5 percent. Norris was teamed with Shepherd. Shepherd wasn't as accurate as Norris (he hit 44 percent from the field), but he scored more points that season (724) than any Butler player before him and broke the single season scoring record with forty-two against DePauw at the fieldhouse.

Shepherd recalled that Tony was very patient with him his sophomore year. He said he made a lot of mistakes and turned the ball over a lot. Tony continued to have his own way of making a player aware: "Coach Hinkle had a 'jackass trophy' that he kept in the locker room for the player who made the most mistakes in a ballgame. About the first five or six games of my sophomore year that trophy had a permanent position on top of my locker, but after that I got the hint and stopped trying to make crazy passes and made the ones I knew the guys could catch." In Shepherd's very first appearance for Hinkle, he scored twenty-six points. It was the opener at Illinois. Hinkle, according to newspaper reports, actually abandoned his traditional pattern attack in that game and replaced it with a lot of free-lancing and dependence on Shepherd. Butler still lost.

Hinkle wasn't about to change his basic game plan drastically, but he did show it wasn't set in concrete. When Butler beat Idaho State it was called a "precision lesson," and when his kids put away Michigan State by twenty-one points it was called a "painful lesson in fundamentals."

For years Hinkle's teams had a standout little man; now on his last team, he had two. Both Norris and Shepherd could hit the basket, move, and handle the ball.

Heading into Hinkle's last game, the Bulldogs were 15–10. Two of those losses were on last-second shots, another one point, still another by two points. Hinkle blamed himself for one of those last-second losses. It was at Rensselaer, his next-to-last game. "We were leading by two," Hinkle recalled, "and I told 'em if St. Joe scored to take the ball to midcourt and then call time, and we'd set up a play. I should have known enough to let them run and shoot." Butler turned the ball over on the set play and St. Joseph's hit the winning bucket, a sixteen-foot jumper at the buzzer. As Tony expressed it, "I masterminded them out of that one." The worst thing about those losses was that they eliminated any postseason tourney bids.

But all that was over and done with. Now Hinkle was just a few minutes away from coaching a Butler basketball team for the last time. He really didn't want it to be the last time, of course. He had quietly wished he could hang on to it all for a while longer—particularly in basketball. In fact, he had applied for the job back in September. But since then he had become convinced that the school felt it was time for him to step down. Once he had made that determination, he knew he wanted no pressure put on the school to keep him. Twelve past presidents of the B-Men's Club had petitioned for his retention as basketball coach. The list included some prestigious figures, representing various decades. On the list were Nipper, Dana Chandler, Cox, Steiner, O'Brien, Doyle, Plump, Dietz. *Indianapolis News*

Sports Editor Wayne Fuson quoted Hinkle on the subject: "Nobody wants to work for somebody who doesn't really want him. This kind of thing [referring to the petition] could cause all kinds of trouble. I love Butler and I wouldn't want that to happen."

Now the familiar voice of Tony's old broadcast colleague Tom Carnegie filled the Hinkle Fieldhouse. Carnegie and Hinkle had been covering the state high school basketball tournament for years on live telecasts fed throughout the state on Channel Six. Carnegie set the tone beautifully that February night when he started the proceedings in typical Carnegie dramatic fashion: "You have your wish, Tony! The fieldhouse named in your honor is full tonight." The crowd responded enthusiastically and another standing ovation followed.

It wasn't all solemnity and emotion. It couldn't be with Carnegie at the microphone. The master of ceremonies relished a presentation that kidded Tony about his lack of interest in the latest clothing styles. Tony seemed to have an endless supply of navy clothing he had purchased before leaving the service—white socks, black shoes, underwear. Style meant nothing to the coach, and Carnegie, knowing his old friend wouldn't be the least bit offended, seized on the subject to lighten up the evening: "White socks are not exactly the 'in' thing. But we know why you wear them. You pick them up in the equipment room for free. And those navy issue shoes you always wear, no doubt you picked up a lifetime supply when you left Great Lakes Naval Training Station. . . . The navy issue white T shirts and shorts have now given you a half-a-lifetime of service." Carnegie then introduced a gentleman wearing the latest attire supplied by an Indianapolis clothing store. Tony was getting some contemporary clothes whether he liked it or not. Tony, incidentally, was wearing his usual gray flannels, blue blazer, and white athletic socks that night.

Notre Dame's athletic director, Moose Krause, was a participant, too. Krause presented Tony with, among other things, an all-expense-paid trip to Hawaii from the Indianapolis Notre Dame Alumni Club. Other presentations came from Indianapolis Mayor Richard Lugar, Indiana Governor Edgar Whitcomb and Butler President Alexander Jones. Jones appeared carrying a large scrapbook filled with telegrams and letters from Butler alumni throughout the United States. Tony found a place for that book in every office he occupied at the school after that night.

Then it was Tony's turn. He needn't have worried about his remarks. The crowd was hushed. He had them in the palm of his hand when he said, "I'd like to think that I've given as much to Indiana, to Indianapolis and to Butler University as they've given to me. . . . Let's make it a happy occasion and hope we have a good game."

Tony got his wish. It was a good game. Butler was still in it with four minutes to go. Then the powerful thirteenth-ranked Irish squad put it away. The Bulldogs couldn't stop Austin Carr. Coach Johnny Dee's phenomenal all-American established a fieldhouse scoring record that night with fifty points. But that wasn't the only record set. Both teams scored more points than any team before them in all the hundreds of games played in the fieldhouse (Notre Dame had 121, Butler 114).

It was a typical run-and-shoot game of the time. Hinkle would have preferred more defense, but months before he had conceded that this team needed to play to its strength, offense. Both Shepherd and Norris had the green light on shot selection from the coach most of the season. That night, Shepherd led the Butler scoring with thirty-eight. Norris broke Butler's free throw shooting percentage record. The team's leading rebounder, Dave Bennett, came through with twelve rebounds and thirty points in a struggle with an extremely physical front line. Also helping the cause was the fact that Notre Dame operated with just seven players. Their six-foot-eight starting center missed the bus and two other players (one a starter) remained on the bench with injuries.

One of Hinkle's team members of long ago accurately summed up the night's proceedings: "It would have been nice if we could have won. But they played the best they could—just like all of Hink's teams. And after all, we came out to say good-by to Hink."

22 Transition and the New Life

Tony Hinkle lost little time after the big finale at the fieldhouse. As he had done so many years before, he moved into preparation for baseball. It started within a few days with indoor workouts and continued until the weather cooperated and Hinkle could get his playing field in shape.

It was not a very satisfying season. His Blue Sox had won just three of fifteen games when he turned the reins over to the newly named athletic director, Tom Warner.

Many years later the Butler baseball record book still showed that a number of Hinkle's kids were still well represented. Six of the top nine single-season batting averages belonged to Hinkle men. The leader was William Shepherd's .418 from 1949. Tom Harding still had the most hits in a game (five in 1938), and Hinkle pitchers were leaders or shared leadership in four categories.

After retirement, golf became an extremely important extracurricular sport for Hinkle. He had played it for years, but now it assisted him in dealing with a personal transition. As Hinkle observed, "I'm really too old to start jogging or lifting weights. So I chase the little ball around, and sometimes I don't have to chase it too far." The Hinkle golf corps consisted of old Butler colleagues Nipper and Dietz along with Bill Hardy, who for years was president of Em Roe Sporting Goods. Hardy had lettered in basketball in the early 1940s. Later he and Hinkle became good friends, a friendship that started out as a business relationship. The foursome played regularly and joined with other B-men frequently. This larger group was known as "the travelers" because they frequently visited other Indiana courses. Buckshot O'Brien and Jerry Cranny were in this latter group.

All during his coaching days at Butler, Hinkle had a definite season for golf. It began the day after the last baseball game and ended on August 15 so he could commit himself strictly to football. That first year of his new status found him still playing into October. Dietz recalled that Tony was complaining late in the day that he was having trouble seeing the ball. He wasn't accustomed to dealing with the low sunlight at that time of year. Of course, his colleagues just let him worry about it for a while.

A few pranks were not uncommon when Hinkle played golf. Sooner or later each of his colleagues got the treatment from the coach. The Friday ritual was golf, then dinner. Hinkle was known to get to a phone now and then during the proceedings and call a participant's wife, asking where her husband was that afternoon since he hadn't shown up for golf. He timed it so that the "accused" would be arriving home shortly thereafter. Somebody decided it was Hinkle's turn. Jerry Cranny was alerted and Hinkle was encouraged to give Jerry the treatment. Hinkle called and went through his usual routine. Two hours or so later Jerry's wife called Hinkle, claiming Jerry still hadn't arrived home. Hinkle got worried and started calling all around, searching for Jerry—who, of course, was at home.

For years Hinkle walked eighteen holes when he played golf. Eventually he walked the front nine and rode the second nine. He shot consistently in the eighties and on occasion got into the upper seventies. He played the game into 1988 when failing eyesight forced him to quit.

By September 1, 1970, the coach was settled into a newly arranged office in Jordan Hall, near the university's director of development, William Powell. Powell was a retired navy captain whose thirty-year military career had led him to Naval Avionics in Indianapolis, his final assignment before retirement to civilian life and a position at Butler. Powell was delighted that Hinkle would be operating in his area of the building. The two hit it off promptly. They could trade navy yarns, and Powell, well schooled in the Hinkle legend, wanted to make sure Tony felt at ease functioning in a different part of the campus.

Butler's public relations director, Chris Theofanis, joined in that effort. He frequently met with Hinkle and Powell for a coffee break at the Union Building. Faculty members started stopping by and suddenly Hinkle was conversing with a whole new crowd. That new crowd was fascinated by the man few really knew. They also found that the coach was quite interested and conversant in matters other than football, basketball, and baseball. He could hold his own in such matters as politics, history, and economics.

Hinkle showed up for work promptly at 8:00 A.M. every day. By late morning he headed either to the fieldhouse for a little conversation down in the locker room or out for a game of golf. If there was a job description for his new title, special assistant to the president, it was broad and pretty much left up to Tony. Generally he was encouraged to attend alumni functions and golf outings and be receptive to speech requests. There were a number of the latter and by this time Tony had begun to enjoy that task. The only other part of the job was to enjoy his less structured life-style.

That was easier said than done, according to family members. He never talked about it, but those close to him felt he was hurt that he hadn't been given the opportunity to coach basketball longer. Close colleagues said he was capable of handling the chore for another five years. But it was not to be, and in time Hinkle settled into a new pattern of life.

He continued to get a lot of attention, of course, from the outside. The B-men, the alumni association, and the Indianapolis Chamber of Commerce teamed up to present a Hinkle testimonial dinner. It was a light-hearted affair that featured remarks by Wayne Fuson, Bob Collins, and Tom Carnegie. Then there was the night Buckshot O'Brien lured him to the annual Boys' Club dinner; to his surprise he was the subject of a local "This Is Your Life" and was presented with the annual Horatio Alger award.

Another change had occurred in Hinkle's life a few years before his departure from coaching. He started turning up at concerts and dances with an old friend, the widow of Tom Joyce. The Hinkles and the Joyces had been friends for many years. Georgette enjoyed music and the arts. Tony had been too preoccupied to pursue that side of life. They began to share each other's interests and to the surprise of some, Tony found he enjoyed dancing. They became regulars at the Indianapolis Athletic Club. It even had an effect on Tony's wardrobe. He was investing in new clothes and giving those black navy shoes a rest. In the years to come Tony and Georgette were regular spectators along with the Dietzes, the Nippers, and others at Butler basketball games. Tony was still seeing Butler compete, but he also was experiencing a new aspect of life and enjoying it.

A Hinkle graduate, George Theofanis, Chris's brother, was now Butler's basketball coach. He had enjoyed success at Shortridge High School and some of his most talented players followed him to Butler. Billy Shepherd, who played his last two years for Theofanis, recalled seeing Hinkle at a distance in the fieldhouse during practice. Shepherd said he could tell that Hinkle missed not running things. He also seemed to be struggling not to appear judgmental.

Happy times at the fieldhouse were far from over for Tony, however. Butler observed the facility's fiftieth year at its opening game of the 1978–79 season. That was combined with the honoring of Tony's 1928–29 team. Eldon Miller's Ohio State Buckeyes were the opposition. That muscular group included sophomore Herb Williams, who later became a member of the Indiana Pacers. It looked like a difficult evening for a while. The visitors led by seventeen at halftime. In the second half, a full-court press helped, as did forward Joe Maloney's ability to hit free throws (sixteen of eighteen). Five-foot-nine Tom Orner won it with a jump shot with three seconds left. The margin was one point. The captain of the 1927–28 team, Archie Chadd, called it some of the old Butler spirit. Team members gathered with Hinkle just before that game for a dinner on campus.

In the 1970s thirteen lucky people signed up for a course at Indiana University–Purdue University at Indianapolis (IUPUI). Its title was "How to Watch Football." The instructor was Tony Hinkle. All those years at Butler, Hinkle had conscientiously continued to teach his classes to undergraduates who were anticipating a teaching or athletic career. This class was for primarily older folks who just wanted to sit and watch and understand the game better.

Hinkle was perfect for the task. He had a knack of keeping his athletes from getting bogged down in complexity. By stressing fundamentals he was saying, let's keep to the basics and remember the uncomplicated purpose of what we're doing. For years people laughed at Hinkle's response to broadcaster Tom Carnegie's question, "Who do you believe will win this basketball game?" Tony's response: "The team that puts the ball in the basket the most times." It was pure Hinkle: subtle, uncomplicated, and true.

In the mid-1970s Hinkle lost another old friend and longtime associate, Butler's athletic trainer for thirty years, James Morris. Jim took the job in the late 1930s one year after graduation. Not only did he help Butler athletes; he also helped a lot of high school athletes who were referred to him by their coaches, many of them Butler graduates. Morris was never too busy to help out.

One of Hinkle's alumni who was having trouble accepting

the death of several friends turned to his old coach one day for advice. "I'll give you a good solution for that," Hinkle said. "When they're here you just have to figure you're winning the game. When they're not here it's just like a game that you've lost. You can't dwell on your losses because if you do you're going to join them."

They rolled out a cake at halftime to observe Hinkle's eightieth birthday when Toledo was the opponent for a Saturday night game in December 1979. Hinkle and lots of his friends were there, but the Bulldogs lost by ten points. Of course, Hinkle was really eighty-one, but the vagueness over the birth date still existed.

Tony undoubtedly had an indirect hand in the decision by the NCAA to bring the finals of the annual basketball tourney to Indianapolis in 1980. It was in Market Square Arena, and it included all the usual fanfare that goes with the Final Four. Every NCAA division I college coach tried to be there and most of them made it. Probably no one knew more of the coaches than Hinkle did and he wasn't about to miss any of it. Louisville came out the winner by five points over UCLA in the Monday night final game.

Hinkle had a remarkable health record at this point despite a habit of heavy smoking. But within a day or two after the tourney he was admitted to St. Vincent Hospital. The diagnosis was pneumonia. Hinkle was exhausted, and the family was convinced he had overextended himself. They feared the worst, but Tony made a comeback and was released after three weeks. He never smoked after that.

Arrangements were made to admit Tony to the Butler University health center for recuperation. Daughter Patty had married David Watson and no longer was living at the West 46th Street home. The family determined that it was time to sell the house and make other living arrangements for Tony. Some six months earlier a heavy rain had caused flooding of the basement and the garage. Much of the coach's memorabilia were lost and his car was beyond repair. Hinkle got another car and moved into the Summit House, an apartment building on the northside of Indianapolis. That would be home for ten years.

By the mid-1980s Hinkle's office was moved back to the fieldhouse, where he found much younger occupants but some familiar faces. Among them were Sylvester, Benbow, Neat, and Joe Sexson, who had been basketball coach since 1977. Hinkle worked out a schedule that took him into the office by 9 A.M.; the work week usually included Saturdays.

When the school observed Tony's eighty-eighth birthday, it was most memorable because for the first time the school had it correct. Tony was indeed eighty-eight in 1986. The other memorable thing was that a whole collection of his kids showed up and lined the periphery of the playing floor at halftime. Tony stepped to the microphone, welcomed them, and thanked them for coming. The Bulldogs then proceeded to defeat Indiana State in four overtimes to make it a perfect afternoon for Butler fans, not to mention Hinkle.

Two years later, on Hinkle's ninetieth birthday, a special issue of the *Butler Collegian* heralded the occasion. Butler again responded by beating Indiana State, this time by fifteen points in regulation time.

In midsummer 1990, Hinkle was still going to his office at Hinkle Fieldhouse. He no longer drove and no longer lived at the Summit House. A student was assigned to pick Tony up every morning at 9:00 Monday through Friday, and he was returned to his new home at the Forum at the Crossing, a retirement community, by noon. He took walks in the afternoon.

Tony still received mail from some of his kids, and some still stopped by to say hello at the fieldhouse. He still went to lunch regularly with people who always kept in touch. Some had played for him, some had coached with him, some had associated with him in various capacities at Butler: Parr, Nipper, Dietz, Powell, Chris Theofanis, Sylvester, just to name a few. The affection and respect of Hinkle grads was a permanent condition. A few years ago Marvin Wood went to see Hinkle because he had something to say to him eyeball to eyeball. He told Hinkle: "Coach, little do you realize the contribution you've made to my life and to that of a lot of other men who've gone through this institution." Hinkle came back with the usual "Oh, kid, anybody would've done that" and Wood told him: "No, Coach, not anyone would've done it and not anyone would've done it the way you did." That's when Wood spotted a couple of tears rolling down Hinkle's cheek.

In 1989–90 the crowds were slim at Butler Bowl for football and at the renovated Hinkle Fieldhouse for basketball. But Tony was there for each game, usually with members of his family. His persistent presence was the result of a condition that came over him in 1921, a condition that was as permanent as Tony's loyalty to the place that hired him and as permanent as the feeling a whole raft of kids have for Tony.

23 Tony in the Nineties

Tony reached the nineties over a year before most of the rest of us. Only for him it was a birthday. For most of the rest of us, it was just another decade.

Hinkle was annoyed about growing older. His eyesight was dimming. His hearing was failing (though a hearing aid helped). His memory was playing tricks on him at times, particularly about recent happenings. But if asked about a player or a moment from his many coaching years, chances were he would remember it clearly. He still had that sense of humor going for him. When one of his grandchildren asked him if he was near-sighted or far-sighted, he responded that he was "no-sighted." One Sunday at a family gathering at the home of one of his daughters, he decided he wanted to go home and asked who was going to take him there. Barbara came back with "nobody." A non–family member who was a guest turned pale. Hinkle jumped to his feet with a smile on his face and declared, "Well, in that case I better start walking."

Butler's old coach still competed. But now it was to keep himself in the mainstream, and one might say he had developed a new Hinkle system. In 1989, when he was approaching his ninety-first birthday, he worried about his ability to pass a driver's test and decided to go on the offense. He initiated a visit to an automobile license branch well ahead of the deadline. The branch was near where he lived. He suggested to the examiner that when it came time for him to drive the examiner might be interested in getting a look at the newly renovated fieldhouse and he would be glad to drive him out there. It was precisely the route Hinkle took six days out of seven. He could almost drive it with his eyes closed. Hinkle passed.

Hinkle's old colleague Bob Dietz, an insurance agent, had handled Hinkle's auto insurance for years. One day he informed the family that, based on Hinkle's driving record of the past few years, he feared a serious accident that might end in a sizable suit against Tony. Dietz said the policy just didn't cover such an expense if that should happen. That was when the family decided Hinkle should no longer drive.

Dietz's concerns were not without cause. Hinkle's failing eyesight had contributed to more than one accident as he was driving back and forth to the fieldhouse. He also had trouble getting into his Summit House parking slot without making contact with supports and leaving dents on the right side of his 1978 Cadillac. Then there was the time he collided with a car parked at the Summit and another when he inflicted a complete loss on a car parked along North Illinois Street.

Hinkle's most spectacular car incident came one day at the fieldhouse parking lot. He had left his headlights on and the battery had been fully recharged for him. He thought the automatic transmission was in park, meaning one move backward would put it in reverse. Unfortunately, the transmission had been left in neutral and the next setting back was drive. Hinkle pulled back and the car took off, headed down the hill toward the Starlight Musicals stage. Before it got there it broke a cable anchored to a large cement section of the stage. The car stopped. Miraculously, Hinkle was not injured in that accident, nor any of the others, and he didn't injure anyone else.

Tony was lucky when it came to general health, too. No one recalled that he ever took a routine physical examination. The closest thing to it during his coaching years was a check by the athletic trainer if he felt any discomfort, which apparently was rare.

Despite his constant effort to avoid spending money, he didn't worry too much about income, at least during periods when he was absorbed in other matters. One time the university treasurer's office called to ask him if he would please cash or deposit his last four paychecks because he was complicating the school's accounting system.

Probably the most amazing aspect of Hinkle was his ability as a young man to figure out his craft—in fact, to master it—and then carry it through successfully for nearly fifty years as a coach. His basic grasp of football and basketball carried him through change after change in the way those games had to be played to remain competitive. He decided early on that the fundamentals were the key to these sports. Mastering the fundamentals meant the ability to adapt to whatever came along. Bob Knight put his finger on what Hinkle was all about in basketball when he read Hinkle this way: "Well, we're going to do things my way. I've got this game figured out and this is how you're going to play it." Hinkle fine tuned along the way with the talent he had to work with and the changes that came with rule alterations, but he never wavered from his basic plan.

Another Hinkle phenomenon was his relationship with the media. He certainly never expected or demanded any special treatment, but one looks long and hard for any criticism of him. He just played it straight. He never exaggerated a point and never avoided a question. One reporter said he was always solid and honest. During the 1960s John Bansch of the *Indianapolis Star* came out with a report critical of Butler in a home basketball game. The next time Hinkle saw John he mentioned that he thought Bansch had been pretty tough on the kids. Bansch replied that he thought it was in order. Hinkle came back with the brief observation: "You know, kid, as long as I've been coaching basketball I still can't figure out whether a bad scoring performance by a team is due to a poor offense or a strong defense." Bansch said he carried that thought into every game he covered after that.

The old athlete still moved pretty well at ninety-one. He rode with Bob Nipper to New Castle in June 1990 to view the newly constructed Indiana Basketball Hall of Fame facility. The two old friends, who shared memories few could match, got a lot of attention that night, and both reveled in it. One of the many people who talked to Tony was Oscar Robertson, the kid who got away.

Tony at ninety-one was having more trouble coming up with names than ever before. But he loved to hear from his Butler kids, many of whom were coping with age problems themselves. And a person had only to look in Hinkle's eyes when one of his kids approached him to know how important all of them still were. And why not? They all shared with their coach a whole gallery of memories.

THE HINKLE STATISTICS

TONY HINKLE'S PERSONAL STAT SHEET

Collegiate Achievements

3 varsity letters each in football, basketball, and baseball, University of Chicago

All-American in basketball, 1920

All-Western Conference (now Big 10) guard in basketball

Coaching Achievements

Butler basketball 1926–42, 1945–70: won 572, lost 403; seventh winningest coach in collegiate history end of 1969–70 season

Butler football 1926, 1934–41, 1946–69: won 171, lost 100, tied 12

Butler baseball 1921–27, 1933–41, 1946–70: won 325, lost 305, tied 4

Great Lakes Naval Training Center basketball 1942–44: won 64, lost 6

Great Lakes Naval Training Center football 1942–43: won 16, lost 5, tied 1

Coach of U.S. team in first U.S.-USSR basketball game in United States

Coach of College All-Star East team, 1969

Coach of Indiana College All-Star team, 1966

Career Achievements

James Naismith Basketball Hall of Fame

Helms Foundation Basketball Hall of Fame (player)

Helms Foundation Basketball Hall of Fame (coach)

Helms Foundation Football Hall of Fame (coach)

Indiana Basketball Hall of Fame

Indiana Football Hall of Fame

National Association of Collegiate Directors of Athletics Hall of Fame

President, National Association of Basketball Coaches, 1954–55

Chairman, NCAA Basketball Rules Committee, 1948–50; member, 1937–38, 1942–50

National Collegiate Basketball Coaches Association Award, 1962

National Association of Basketball Coaches Golden Anniversary Award, 1986

The Hinkle Statistics

HINKLE-BUTLER FOOTBALL SEASONS

*denotes Indiana Collegiate Conference Champion

1926

Butler	Opponent	Opp.
38	Earlham	0
70	Hanover	0
7	Illinois	38
7	Franklin	0
10	DePauw	21
0	Lombard	18
0	Wabash	13
0	Minnesota	81
6	Dayton	30

1934

Butler	Opponent	Opp.
13	Ball State	4
25	Franklin	0
50	Central Normal	0
12	Indiana State	0
0	Wabash	0
7	Washington (St. Louis)	32
6	Manchester	0
12	Valparaiso	7

1935

Butler	Opponent	Opp.
29	Louisville	0
12	Evansville	0
71	Hanover	7
33	Indiana State	7
39	Valparaiso	0
20	Wabash	0
18	Franklin	0
7	Western State	19

1936

Butler	Opponent	Opp.
40	Evansville	0
12	Cincinnati	12
6	Chicago	6
26	Manchester	0
9	Wabash	7
64	Franklin	0
41	Valparaiso	0
13	Western State	7

1937

Butler	Opponent	Opp.
7	Purdue	33
13	Cincinnati	0
33	Valparaiso	0
51	Evansville	0
12	Washington & Jefferson	0
12	DePauw	0
0	Wabash	0
13	Western State	14

1938

Butler	Opponent	Opp.
12	Ball State	6
6	Purdue	21
0	George Washington	26
12	DePauw	0
35	Ohio Wesleyan	0
27	Wabash	0
0	Western State	13
21	Washington (St. Louis)	27

The Hinkle Statistics

1939

16	Ball State	0
12	Ohio	7
34	Indiana State	0
13	George Washington	6
33	DePauw	0
6	Washington (St. Louis)	6
55	Wabash	0
12	Western State	0

1940

27	St. Joseph's	6
0	Purdue	28
7	Ohio	7
6	Xavier (Cincinnati)	13
19	Wabash	12
19	Washington (St. Louis)	27
32	DePauw	6
26	Ball State	0
6	Toledo	20

1941

6	St. Joseph's	13
7	Xavier (Cincinnati)	40
6	Western Michigan	14
13	Ball State	6
20	DePauw	6
7	Ohio	20
26	Wabash	0
18	Toledo	2
40	Washington (St. Louis)	13

1946

19	Eastern Illinois State	12
13	Indiana State	7
0	Western Michigan	19
41	DePauw	6
20	Ball State	6
25	Wabash	7
31	St. Joseph's	6
25	Valparaiso	0

1947

6	Ball State	6
7	Ohio	14
21	St. Joseph's	0
14	Wabash	0
21	Western Michigan	20
35	DePauw	0
0	Western Reserve	6
27	Valparaiso	6
19	Cincinnati	26

1948

68	Indiana Central	7
14	Evansville	13
0	Western Reserve	6
0	Washington (St. Louis)	7
7	Cincinnati	16
20	Wabash	7
7	Western Michigan	20
6	Ohio	14

The Hinkle Statistics

1949

7	Evansville	24
14	Wabash	7
6	Western Reserve	28
47	Indiana State	14
0	Washington (St. Louis)	7
0	Illinois Normal	14
6	Western Michigan	40
0	Ohio	14

1950

12	Evansville	14
7	Wabash	7
14	Ohio	21
33	Ball State	7
7	Miami (Ohio)	42
25	Western Reserve	14
13	Western Michigan	34
25	Washington (St. Louis)	20
32	Indiana State	0

1951

7	Valparaiso	41
7	Western Reserve	6
26	Wabash	26
20	Ball State	14
6	St. Joseph's	12
27	Evansville	12
0	Western Michigan	20
13	Washington (St. Louis)	20
14	Indiana State	7

1952*

25	Evansville	20
47	North Central (Ill.)	6
25	Wabash	27
28	Ball State	6
33	St. Joseph's	0
13	Indiana State	13
13	Valparaiso	14
33	Washington (St. Louis)	20
14	Western Reserve	42

1953*

27	Evansville	0
24	Wabash	20
25	Ball State	7
47	St. Joseph's	13
47	Indiana State	12
32	Valparaiso	20
14	Washington (St. Louis)	27
20	Western Reserve	21

1954

21	Evansville	14
14	Wabash	21
13	Ball State	26
40	St. Joseph's	12
38	Indiana State	26
7	Valparaiso	39
6	Washington (St. Louis)	25
13	Indiana Central	7
13	Western Reserve	13

The Hinkle Statistics

1955

14	Evansville	45
26	Indiana State	19
20	Ball State	13
13	St. Joseph's	28
18	DePauw	7
14	Valparaiso	24
12	Wabash	14
20	Washington (St. Louis)	41

1956

34	Evansville	7
32	Indiana State	0
28	Ball State	12
6	St. Joseph's	31
19	DePauw	13
20	Valparaiso	6
26	Wabash	7
20	Washington (St. Louis)	21

1957

0	Bradley	13
14	Wabash	6
13	St. Joseph's	34
27	Indiana State	0
27	Valparaiso	0
27	Ball State	7
19	Evansville	7
26	DePauw	13
41	Washington (St. Louis)	13

1958*

39	Bradley	19
40	Wabash	6
6	St. Joseph's	0
31	Indiana State	8
34	Valparaiso	0
7	Ball State	14
28	Evansville	14
30	DePauw	0
20	Washington (St. Louis)	12

1959*

27	Bradley	8
28	Wabash	8
20	St. Joseph's	7
41	Indiana State	6
10	Valparaiso	7
27	Ball State	0
33	Evansville	14
21	DePauw	3
48	Washington (St. Louis)	13

1960*

18	Bradley	12
40	Wabash	7
6	St. Joseph's	24
20	Indiana State	13
27	Valparaiso	20
27	Ball State	0
34	Evansville	6
13	DePauw	6
33	Washington (St. Louis)	6

1961*

34	Bradley	23
48	Ball State	6
34	Wabash	7
12	DePauw	6
27	St. Joseph's	7
26	Indiana State	0
14	Valparaiso	2
30	Evansville	7
26	Washington (St. Louis)	7

1962*

34	Bradley	16
28	Ball State	28
14	Wabash	14
21	DePauw	18
0	St. Joseph's	6
41	Indiana State	20
16	Valparaiso	14
41	Evansville	0
13	Marshall	26

1963*

13	Morehead State	31
35	Bradley	27
13	Ball State	0
26	Wabash	21
14	DePauw	12
27	St. Joseph's	0
7	Indiana State	6
20	Valparaiso	12
32	Evansville	14

1964*

7	Morehead State	26
21	Bradley	28
14	Ball State	28
7	Wabash	7
9	DePauw	6
41	St. Joseph's	0
7	Indiana State	2
14	Valparaiso	23
48	Evansville	21

1965

41	Taylor	6
27	Indiana State	7
21	St. Joseph's	12
21	Valparaiso	23
42	Evansville	0
7	Ball State	22
14	DePauw	8
7	Akron	14
27	Western Kentucky	20

1966

6	Northern Illinois	34
28	Indiana State	6
20	St. Joseph's	7
12	Valparaiso	15
26	Evansville	7
14	Ball State	17
14	DePauw	7
14	Akron	20
7	Western Kentucky	35

The Hinkle Statistics

1967

7	Northern Illinois	24
7	Indiana State	23
27	St. Joseph's	2
7	Valparaiso	21
7	Evansville	24
7	Ball State	65
20	DePauw	21
14	Wabash	0
14	Western Kentucky	36

1968

7	Akron	32
0	Bowling Green (Ky.)	35
12	Indiana State	28
49	St. Joseph's	14
7	Valparaiso	10
7	Evansville	44
21	Ball State	24
7	DePauw	30
26	Wabash	9

1969

0	Akron	52
57	Indiana Central	0
7	Ball State	36
34	DePauw	23
6	Wabash	17
17	St. Joseph's	20
31	Indiana State	54
9	Evansville	14
38	Valparaiso	20

HINKLE-BUTLER FOOTBALL RECORD AGAINST MAJOR OPPONENTS

	W	L	T
Akron	0	4	
Ball State	17	8	2
Bradley	6	2	
DePauw	20	3	
Evansville	19	6	
Franklin	4	0	
Indiana Central	3	0	
Indiana State	21	3	1
Ohio	1	5	1
Purdue	0	3	
St. Joseph's	15	8	
Valparaiso	16	9	
Wabash	20	5	6
Washington (St. Louis)	8	10	
Western Kentucky	1	3	
Western Michigan	3	9	
Western State	2	5	1

HINKLE-GREAT LAKES NAVAL TRAINING CENTER FOOTBALL

1942

0	Michigan	9
25	Iowa	0
7	Pittsburgh	6
7	Wisconsin	13
0	Michigan State	14
17	Missouri	0
42	Purdue	0
24	Marquette	0
6	Illinois	0
13	Notre Dame	13

1943

20	Ft. Riley (Kansas)	19
13	Purdue	23
21	Iowa	7
40	Pittsburgh	0
13	Ohio State	6
0	Northwestern	13
41	Marquette	7
32	Western Michigan	6
12	Camp Grant (Ill.)	0
21	Indiana	7
25	Marquette	6
19	Notre Dame	14

HINKLE FOOTBALL LETTERMEN WHO COACHED HIGH SCHOOL OR COLLEGE TEAMS

(C) denotes a team captain

Alenduff, Marty 1964
Anthony, Jim 1969
Armstrong, Scott 1933–34
Bailey, Van 1964–67
Barr, Richard 1949
Batts, Roscoe 1933–35
Belden, Jim 1962–64*
Benbow, Don 1959–61 (C)
Boa, Andy 1935–37
Bopp, Ed 1966–68 (C)
Bork, Bill 1957–59
Brock, Bob 1967–69
Brown, Leonard 1969–71
Burdette, Cody 1935–36
Caporale, Edgio 1958–59
Caporale, Louis 1954
Chandler, Scott 1953–55
Chelminiak, John 1948–50
Conley, Bob 1968
Cosgrove, Walter 1932
Craver, Jim 1966–68
Crumley, Jim 1950–51
Dezelan, Joseph 1938–40 (C)
Dezelan, Joseph, Jr. 1964–65
Dimancheff, Boris 1941–42
Disney, James 1966
Dold, Leslie 1942, 1946
Downham, Bob 1963–64
Dullaghan, Dick 1963–65**
Ellenberger, Norm 1951–53 (C)
Enright, Dave 1963–65
Fish, Guy 1950–51 (C)
Freeman, Ken 1960–61
Gallagher, Dan 1959, 1961

Gerlach, Les 1951–54
Goens, Larry 1959–61
Gollner, Bob 1951
Guyer, Dick 1947
Hamilton, Bob 1942, 1946–48
Hamman, Bruce 1950–51
Harding, Tom 1937–39
Hauss, Craig 1965–66
Hauss, Jim 1936–37
Hoffman, Mark 1969–71
Holok, Al 1967–69
Horvath, Steve 1947
Hurrle, Ott 1946–48 (C)
Johnson, Charles 1951–52 (C)
Kokinda, Jack 1967
Kuntz, Bill, Sr. 1946–49 (C)
Kyvik, Curtis 1946–49
Landry, Virgil 1950–51
Laymon, Clarence 1933–35 (C)
Leamon, Charles 1948
Leffler, Jim 1968–69
Leffler, Ken 1963–65
Macek, Joseph 1935, 1937
Mahoney, Leo 1952–55
Manka, John 1950–51
McGinley, Mike 1961–63***
McNerney, Chester 1933
Mitschelem, Lyle 1962–64 (C)
Moriarity, Francis 1942, 1946–48 (C)
Moses, John 1956–58
Murphy, John 1946–49
Niemeyer, John 1966–68
Nolan, Dan 1968–70
Oberting, Dave 1961
Pedigo, Bob 1956–57
Peebles, Julian 1967
Perrone, Mel 1941–42, 1946
Peterson, David 1947–49
Potter, Wally 1941–42, 1946 (C)
Purichia, Joe 1964–65
Purkhiser, Bob 1938–40
Rabold, John 1937, 1939–40
Ratliff, Vern 1960–61
Reisler, Phil 1939
Renie, Tim 1961–62
Rosenstihl, James 1947
Sells, Tom 1958
Sheridan, Hansel 1960–62
Shook, Larry 1960–62
Skirchak, John 1958–60
Sleet, Tom 1941–42, 1946–47
Steinmetz, Mark 1965–66
Stout, Waldo 1934–36
Swift, Cliff 1934–36
Sylvester, Bill 1946–49
Sypult, Gene 1950, 1953
Thompson, Wes 1962–63
Tinder, Ed 1969–70
Vandermeer, Mel 1937–39
Vlasic, Jerry 1957, 1959
Walls, Wayne 1951–52 (C)
Weesner, Ron 1957
Welton, Frank 1936–38

*Carmel High School AAA State Champion 1980, 1981, AAAA State Champion 1986, 1989

**Carmel High School AAA State Champion 1978; Ben Davis H.S. AAAAA State Champion 1987, 1988

***Indianapolis Cathedral AAA State Champion 1986

HINKLE-BUTLER BASKETBALL SEASONS

*denotes Hoosier Classic game; ** denotes NIT postseason game; *** denotes NCAA postseason game; **** denotes Indiana Collegiate Conference Champion

1926–27

28	Central Normal	24
29	Coe (Iowa)	25
27	Illinois Wesleyan	21
24	Lombard (Ill.)	25
30	Chicago	28
40	Muncie Normal	38
23	Evansville	25
33	Marquette	30
53	Michigan State	16
30	DePauw	25
49	Iowa	32
29	Michigan State	23
27	Western State Normal	34
32	Illinois	30
29	Franklin	26
27	Evansville	35
40	Wabash	22
40	DePauw	33
35	Marquette	23
38	Franklin	31
32	Wabash	30

17-4

1927–28

49	Central Normal	22
18	Wisconsin	25
50	Concordia	10
27	Purdue	36
39	Muncie Normal	34
25	Chicago	24
38	Evansville (double OT)	32
42	NAGU	26
40	Franklin	32
33	Evansville	27
36	DePauw	19
34	Danville Normal	25
28	Wabash	26
23	Marquette	20
27	Loyola	17
24	Notre Dame	32
29	Franklin	21
35	Wabash	22
53	Marquette	15
32	DePauw	27
21	Notre Dame	13

18-3

The Hinkle Statistics

1928–29			1929–30		
35	Pittsburgh	33	53	Manchester	22
28	Purdue	27	20	NAGU	17
35	Danville Normal	22	36	Purdue	29
47	North Carolina	24	49	Montana State	32
38	Missouri	25	39	Vanderbilt	14
21	Chicago	24	16	Central Normal	40
34	Franklin	26	38	Nebraska	26
56	Evansville	10	28	Illinois	18
35	DePauw	20	28	Chicago	21
67	Indiana Central	19	32	Wabash	15
40	Evansville	31	20	Franklin	34
33	Illinois	28	27	Central Normal	19
32	Wabash (OT)	28	39	DePauw	29
41	Franklin	33	14	Loyola	22
21	Notre Dame	24	14	Wabash	16
34	DePauw	23	20	Notre Dame	28
47	Earlham	19	31	Earlham	27
27	Wabash	22	16	Notre Dame	29
35	Notre Dame	16	28	Franklin	31
17-2	National Collegiate Champion		12–7		

The Hinkle Statistics

1930–31

36	Cincinnati	12
45	Brigham Young	34
27	Loyola	22
23	Alabama	20
37	Arkansas	21
35	State Normal	23
33	Louisville	16
30	Wabash	30
31	Western State	28
24	Evansville	17
30	Concordia	23
14	Nebraska	32
34	Centenary (Louisiana)	16
25	Franklin	18
38	Louisville	16
19	Notre Dame	27
23	Wabash	18
19	Franklin	14
20	Notre Dame	15

17–2

1931–32

22	Evansville	19
36	Southern Calif.	16
23	Pittsburgh	20
22	Illinois	17
38	Hanover	11
28	Montana	17
19	Loyola	21
27	Central Normal	19
34	Wabash	11
39	Western State	19
37	Franklin	28
31	State Normal	35
36	Ball State	22
17	Wisconsin	28
32	Notre Dame	37
38	Franklin	23
35	Central Normal	27
23	Wabash	16
23	Notre Dame	28

14–5

The Hinkle Statistics

1932–33

21	Indiana State	40
30	Missouri	23
30	Pittsburgh	38
41	Western State	38
32	Central Normal	41
36	Drake	12
56	Grinnell	22
31	Wabash	27
27	Notre Dame	25
31	Oklahoma A&M	18
47	Franklin	28
26	Oklahoma A&M	21
25	Creighton	35
34	Washington (Missouri)	32
33	Washington	27
46	Grinnell	15
37	Wabash	20
40	Franklin	32
45	Creighton	33
43	Drake	21
41	Notre Dame (OT)	42

16–5
Missouri Valley Conference
Champion

1933–34

31	Indiana Central	32
34	Franklin	22
35	Pittsburgh	24
34	Purdue	37
27	Wisconsin	37
24	Indiana State	20
42	Washington (Missouri)	26
17	Notre Dame	37
35	Franklin	27
48	Creighton	30
35	Wabash	32
36	Grinnell	24
28	Drake	18
33	Creighton	32
24	Grinnell	26
38	Oklahoma A&M	26
49	Oklahoma A&M	26
24	Notre Dame	34
39	Drake	27
24	Wabash	31
53	Washington	47

14–7
Missouri Valley Conference
Champion

The Hinkle Statistics

1934–35

44	Earlham	29
37	Indiana Central	24
24	Pittsburgh	42
31	Purdue	34
39	Illinois	24
36	Northwestern	41
37	Chicago	31
37	Franklin	19
30	Wabash	24
29	Notre Dame	30
43	Loyola	25
41	Valparaiso	25
54	Indiana State	40
56	Western Reserve	39
39	Franklin	23
50	Western State	39
51	Central Normal	32
22	Wabash	28
23	Notre Dame	27
31	Indiana State	47

13–7

1935–36

34	Indiana Central	39
38	Franklin	29
28	Pittsburgh	36
41	Purdue	39
39	Cincinnati	26
23	Michigan	26
43	Wabash	30
35	Earlham	41
27	Notre Dame	35
32	Detroit	38
24	Michigan State	21
39	Western State	42
38	Marquette	35
24	Wisconsin	28
38	Northwestern	53
28	Kentucky	39
26	Central Normal	27
32	Wabash	35
35	Indiana State	37
37	Franklin	38
30	Notre Dame	34
40	Augustana (Olympic Trials)	41

6–16

The Hinkle Statistics

1936–37

27	Earlham	33
21	Pittsburgh	33
14	Purdue	44
27	Indiana Central	41
43	Wisconsin	23
27	Indiana	61
27	Michigan	36
24	Notre Dame	25
28	DePauw	29
26	Xavier (Ohio)	28
29	Marquette	26
27	Franklin	30
26	Wabash	13
28	Central Normal	32
27	Michigan State	21
32	Franklin	37
30	Wabash	24
26	DePauw	27
32	Indiana State (OT)	28
17	Notre Dame	42

6–14

1937–38

45	Oakland City	26
28	Louisville	23
24	Pittsburgh	23
31	Iowa	36
30	Northwestern	21
38	Boston	33
38	Cincinnati	25
38	Michigan	35
32	Marquette	39
32	DePauw	28
15	Central Normal	22
40	Indiana Central	43
26	Notre Dame	39
15	Michigan State	21
21	Detroit	25
23	Indiana	42
25	Wabash	22
26	Franklin	39
20	Marquette	25
22	Notre Dame	45
40	DePauw	24
28	Wabash	38
32	Franklin	30

11–12

The Hinkle Statistics

1938–39

44	Valparaiso	26
31	Iowa	29
24	Wisconsin	21
29	Indiana	46
31	Michigan	40
36	Marquette	43
35	Notre Dame	37
54	DePauw	27
46	Franklin	41
34	Michigan State	33
24	Detroit	33
29	Michigan State	39
39	DePauw	29
31	Franklin	24
27	Wabash	25
37	Indiana Central	33
41	St. Joseph's	29
46	DePauw	39
42	Wabash	16
35	Notre Dame	27

14–6

1939–40

29	Ball State	23
47	Pittsburgh	36
35	Iowa	32
33	Indiana	40
42	Southern Methodist	37
18	Illinois	37
44	Long Island	46
46	La Salle	37
49	Franklin	35
47	DePauw	21
39	Notre Dame	55
41	Detroit	35
47	Wabash	26
43	Loyola	39
61	Franklin	43
45	Ohio State	51
50	Wisconsin	46
30	Northwestern	32
38	CCNY	36
43	Marquette	32
31	Wabash	27
56	DePauw	25
39	Notre Dame	38

17–6

1940–41

36	Indiana	39
51	Ohio State	49
32	Northwestern	31
25	Michigan	32
40	Pittsburgh	41
32	DePaul	53
57	Xavier (Ohio)	33
35	Notre Dame	45
38	DePauw	34
45	Franklin	32
38	Ball State	36
35	Long Island	46
43	St. Joseph's (Philadelphia)	47
52	Ohio State	30
41	Wabash	35
37	Marquette	41
55	Wisconsin	59
40	Marquette	38
33	DePauw	28
34	Wabash	30
54	Notre Dame	40
38	Franklin	34

13–9

1941–42

50	Franklin	40
40	Northwestern	46
50	Illinois	52
41	Iowa	35
39	Pittsburgh	29
34	Purdue	50
45	Michigan	37
35	Oregon State	29
40	Great Lakes	51
34	Wabash	29
29	Marquette	39
41	DePauw	34
49	Notre Dame	43
38	Ball State	36
39	Michigan State	40
37	Chanute Field	32
43	Franklin	31
38	Michigan State	36
30	Marquette	40
35	Wabash	42
32	DePauw	28
54	Notre Dame	57

13–9

The Hinkle Statistics

1945–46

48	Manchester	43
45	Wabash	35
45	Illinois Wesleyan	52
47	Ball State	40
47	Miami (Ohio)	40
48	DePauw	44
41	Louisville	51
37	Miami (Ohio)	35
47	Indiana	58
42	Earlham	40
73	Illinois Wesleyan	50
38	Wabash	36
45	DePauw	49
50	Valparaiso	55
40	Franklin	37
62	Earlham	53
35	Ball State	60
33	Louisville	79
49	Valparaiso	85
61	Franklin	48

12–8

1946–47

52	Wisconsin	60
41	Pittsburgh	39
58	Cincinnati	53
59	Canterbury	54
40	Northwestern	44
52	Indiana	41
77	Western Reserve	60
40	Notre Dame	86
65	DePauw	61
56	Western Reserve	53
55	Valparaiso	43
54	Ohio State	50
79	Wayne State	26
80	Ohio	70
60	Notre Dame	73
53	Wabash	40
68	Valparaiso	44
63	Wabash	49
39	DePauw	49
56	Purdue	48
57	Wayne State	49
53	Ohio	62
51	Cincinnati	61

16–7

The Hinkle Statistics

1947–48

51	Northwestern	52
53	Wisconsin	61
67	St. Joseph's	49
52	Canterbury	30
52	Purdue	50*
64	Indiana	51*
47	Notre Dame	71
62	Wabash	38
67	DePauw	42
61	Valparaiso	45
57	Ohio State	47
53	Cincinnati	72
59	Ohio	35
52	Notre Dame	53
70	Western Reserve	40
31	Wabash	46
56	Cincinnati	58
61	Valparaiso	57
49	DePauw	43
61	Western Reserve	50

14–7

1948–49

62	Illinois	67
48	Ohio State	60
52	Indiana State	49
59	Wabash	35
63	Long Island	54
64	Indiana	55*
47	Purdue	43*
42	Indiana Central	39
63	DePauw	36
59	Miami (Ohio)	38
74	Cincinnati	52
58	Notre Dame	60
54	Ohio	53
53	Miami (Ohio)	48
68	Notre Dame	54
72	Ohio	41
51	Wabash	42
88	Western Michigan	52
56	DePauw	49
79	Western Reserve	42
44	Cincinnati	49
70	Western Michigan	58
61	Western Reserve	66

18–5

The Hinkle Statistics

1949–50

56	Illinois	60
65	Ohio State	67
48	Michigan	73
55	Wabash	49
53	Evansville	48
57	Purdue	52*
57	Indiana	68*
33	Notre Dame	54
50	DePauw	49
48	Miami (Ohio)	50
70	Western Reserve	56
49	Indiana	57
56	Cincinnati	64
63	Notre Dame	57
51	Wabash	42
70	Ohio	49
76	Western Reserve	46
62	DePauw	64
68	Western Michigan	49
53	Cincinnati	55
48	Miami (Ohio)	46
57	Western Michigan	70
67	Ohio	56
65	Ohio State	66

12–12

1950–51

50	Ohio State	72
60	Northwestern	70
54	Iowa	51
49	Wabash	54
37	Michigan	58
46	Indiana	61*
59	Purdue	65*
61	Evansville	82
52	Illinois	88
37	Evansville	52
48	Notre Dame	55
59	Ball State	54
63	St. Joseph's	48
58	Wabash	57
52	Indiana State	56
60	Valparaiso	64
65	Notre Dame	75
35	Wisconsin	60
76	Valparaiso	80
46	Indiana State	65
53	DePauw	61
63	St. Joseph's	55
46	Ball State	65
36	DePauw	46

5–19

The Hinkle Statistics

1951–52****

57	Northwestern	93
57	Illinois	68
70	Ohio State	74
63	Michigan	53
58	Wabash	60
51	Purdue	55*
71	Indiana	87*
73	Evansville	58
68	DePauw	61
49	Notre Dame	55
52	Indiana State (OT)	54
77	Wabash	66
51	Valparaiso	49
71	Evansville	65
57	Iowa	58
60	Wisconsin	62
61	Ball State	57
48	Notre Dame	52
51	Indiana State	49
89	St. Joseph's	48
70	DePauw	55
55	Valparaiso	75
60	St. Joseph's	54
59	Ball State	46

12–12

1952–53****

52	Iowa	62
67	Purdue	61
63	Ohio State	60
58	Illinois	75
72	Northwestern	90
47	Notre Dame	63
67	Michigan	63
74	Evansville	61
93	DePauw	68
65	Wabash	53
78	Indiana State	64
57	St. Joseph's	72
80	Valparaiso	74
77	Wabash	58
74	Evansville	70
70	Indiana	105
58	Notre Dame	80
82	Ball State	52
51	Indiana State	56
85	St. Joseph's	64
75	DePauw	67
75	Valparaiso	53
54	Ball State	77

14–9

The Hinkle Statistics

1953–54****

54	Wisconsin	70
78	Ohio State	93
48	Illinois	80
57	Indiana	76
67	Purdue	65
81	Michigan	77
71	Wabash	63
57	Northwestern	70
68	Rio Grande (Ohio)	81
77	Wabash	75
74	DePauw	64
53	Evansville	64
49	Indiana State	60
78	Northwestern	60
87	Valparaiso	67
85	St. Joseph's	59
58	Notre Dame	95
67	Valparaiso	87
75	Ball State	73
79	Evansville	67
85	Indiana State	70
73	DePauw	83
56	Notre Dame	81
65	Valparaiso	63
78	Ball State	75

13–12

1954–55

34	Illinois	88
80	Ohio State	98
79	Wabash	67
56	Michigan	71
54	Purdue	82
83	Northwestern	62
74	Northwestern	81
58	Notre Dame	83
76	DePauw	52
62	Wabash	83
72	Indiana State	59
75	Evansville	73
53	Wisconsin	57
49	St. Joseph's	72
57	Valparaiso	67
56	Indiana	87
75	Evansville	83
75	Ball State	73
80	St. Joseph's	72
79	Indiana State	60
71	Notre Dame	81
68	DePauw	47
80	Valparaiso	67
65	Ball State	83

10–14

The Hinkle Statistics

1955–56

67	Wisconsin	63
51	Ohio State	73
75	Illinois	107
86	Wabash	63
63	Michigan	57
59	Purdue	67
70	Indiana	94
89	Princeton	71
69	Notre Dame	83
72	DePauw	68
75	St. Joseph's	77
77	Evansville (OT)	82
66	Indiana State	64
69	Ball State	59
77	Evansville	93
89	Valparaiso	66
40	Valparaiso	63
81	Notre Dame	64
84	Wabash	70
87	Indiana State	73
77	DePauw	69
74	St. Joseph's	58
84	Ball State	74

14–9

1956–57

82	Ohio State	98
54	Wisconsin	50
81	Illinois	98
80	Wabash	53
68	Indiana	73
77	Michigan	84
83	Michigan State (OT)	79
79	Purdue	83
71	UCLA	82
72	Denver	69
86	Notre Dame	84
67	St. Joseph's	83
89	Evansville	87
70	DePauw	64
92	Indiana State	74
72	Evansville	81
67	St. Joseph's	68
67	Valparaiso	78
79	Ball State	68
67	Wabash	77
65	Notre Dame	70
61	Valparaiso	50
55	Indiana State	67
77	DePauw	68
67	Ball State	78

11–14

1957–58

55	Michigan State	74
90	Fort Knox	64
77	Ohio State	73
75	Illinois	91
73	Wabash	63
58	Wisconsin	59
85	Michigan	65
84	Indiana	78*
78	Purdue	83*
75	Fresno State	85
72	Notre Dame	83
62	St. Joseph's	64
101	Evansville	76
70	DePauw	64
91	Indiana State	71
85	Evansville (OT)	89
89	St. Joseph's	81
83	Valparaiso	63
91	Ball State	79
79	Wabash	68
81	Notre Dame	90
81	Valparaiso	73
93	Indiana State (double OT)	87
76	DePauw	60
82	Ball State (OT)	76
69	St. John's (N.Y.)	76**

16–10

1958–59****

79	Illinois	103
55	Wabash	56
46	Michigan State	72
70	Michigan	86
69	Ohio State	81
79	Dartmouth (OT)	74
81	Tennessee	66
65	Purdue	78*
81	Indiana	76*
69	Wisconsin	55
59	Navy	58
62	Notre Dame	60
78	Evansville	75
73	DePauw	61
56	Indiana State	54
78	Evansville (OT)	85
86	St. Joseph's	76
79	Wabash	68
65	Valparaiso	64
77	Ball State	67
88	St. Joseph's	75
80	Valparaiso	68
92	Notre Dame (triple OT)	89
87	Indiana State (double OT)	88
76	DePauw	68
85	Ball State	73
94	Fordham	80**
77	Bradley	83**

19–9

The Hinkle Statistics

1959–60

88	Wisconsin	82
75	Illinois	83
62	Wabash	55
66	Ohio State	99
85	Michigan	63
68	Ohio State	96
79	UCLA	73
85	Indiana	91*
73	Purdue	69*
80	Michigan State	85
66	Bradley	86
51	Notre Dame	76
50	Evansville	71
79	DePauw	67
82	Indiana State	52
105	St. Joseph's	97
92	St. Joseph's	60
108	Wabash (5 OT)	110
74	Valparaiso	60
73	Ball State	56
69	Evansville	86
89	Valparaiso	72
62	Notre Dame	79
84	Indiana State	66
69	DePauw	66
100	Ball State	72

15–11

1960–61****

73	Wisconsin	58
71	Michigan State (OT)	77
52	Illinois	84
68	Michigan	56
65	Bradley	71
56	Southern California	66
61	UCLA	73
61	Wabash	68
70	Illinois	68*
65	Purdue	63*
71	Yale	64
56	Notre Dame	72
93	Evansville	82
77	DePauw	72
93	Indiana State	67
73	St. Joseph's	63
107	St. Joseph's	64
69	Notre Dame	74
90	Valparaiso	81
82	Ball State	73
61	Wabash	74
74	Evansville	92
95	Valparaiso	74
71	Indiana State	74
83	DePauw	65
73	Ball State	59

15–11

The Hinkle Statistics

1961–62****

72	Illinois	82
77	New Mexico State	56
69	Michigan	61
80	Bradley	77
57	Purdue	65
69	DePauw	85
72	Michigan State	77
73	Illinois Wesleyan	65
74	Toledo	61
63	Princeton	58
75	Evansville	66
83	Notre Dame	67
68	Wabash	49
78	Indiana State	75
76	St. Joseph's	65
89	St. Joseph's	55
92	Valparaiso	70
61	Ball State	58
90	Wabash	67
92	Evansville	87
52	Valparaiso	60
86	Notre Dame	77
63	Indiana State	61
80	DePauw	72
87	Ball State	86
56	Bowling Green	55***
60	Kentucky	81***
87	Western Kentucky (consolation)	86***

22–6

1962–63

49	Illinois	66
57	Toledo	73
74	Utah State	80
70	Michigan	69
81	Bradley	87
78	Purdue	93
68	UCLA	81
66	Notre Dame	59
62	Ohio State	66
89	Dartmouth	55
70	St. Joseph's	61
82	Valparaiso	58
56	Indiana State	76
75	Wabash	54
54	Notre Dame	80
77	Ball State	60
70	DePauw	59
70	Southern Illinois	58
69	Indiana State	65
60	Evansville	78
74	Ball State	66
78	St. Joseph's	56
75	Valparaiso	58
92	Wabash	60
79	Evansville	74
79	DePauw	71

16–10

The Hinkle Statistics

1963–64

52	Illinois	59
68	Ohio State	74
62	Southern California	74
65	UCLA	80
70	Michigan	80
65	Purdue	59
53	Illinois	74
82	Toledo	61
65	Michigan State	76
67	St. Joseph's	62
95	Valparaiso	84
69	Indiana State	61
80	Wabash	52
79	Ball State	74
89	DePauw	64
68	Bradley	77
80	Indiana State	61
64	Notre Dame	72
73	Evansville	83
73	Ball State	90
76	Wabash	67
78	St. Joseph's	62
83	Valparaiso	76
73	Notre Dame	90
61	Evansville	70
73	DePauw	71

13–13

1964–65

93	Wabash	80
84	Utah State	88
66	Utah	95
66	Ohio State	67
64	Purdue	80
90	Michigan State	89
84	Tulane	67
81	Michigan	99
62	Toledo	84
79	Akron	58
88	DePauw	90
71	Evansville	79
79	St. Joseph's	72
90	Wabash	70
72	Ball State	85
57	Notre Dame	94
80	Bradley	74
74	Indiana State	81
99	St. Joseph's	84
74	Valparaiso	80
72	Notre Dame	94
85	Valparaiso	69
73	Evansville	84
85	Indiana State	87
102	Ball State	97
115	DePauw	97

11–15

The Hinkle Statistics

1965–66

74	Illinois	88
77	Southern California	75
74	Ohio State	75
56	Michigan State	75
77	Purdue	84
70	Bradley	73
76	Indiana State	70
79	Michigan	64
65	Oklahoma	63
89	Toledo	79
75	Yale	67
86	St. Joseph's	65
68	Evansville	104
101	Wabash	73
83	Valparaiso	89
75	Ball State	71
107	DePauw	63
90	Notre Dame	67
90	Indiana State	108
110	Evansville	83
61	Notre Dame	84
93	Valparaiso	91
96	Wabash	71
65	Ball State	75
99	St. Joseph's	84
83	DePauw	69

16–10

1966–67

67	Ohio State	74
51	Illinois	82
97	Wisconsin-Milwaukee	86
98	Purdue	99
80	Michigan	91
68	Western Kentucky	81
81	Northern Illinois	70
78	Bradley	74
87	National Club Champions (Sweden)	68
76	Toledo	87
64	Cornell	69
95	Ball State	93
73	Valparaiso	102
89	Wabash	71
63	St. Joseph's	59
71	Evansville	75
75	Indiana State	83
84	St. Joseph's	71
80	Notre Dame	101
76	DePauw	80
71	Wabash	81
82	Valparaiso	72
71	Ball State	72
48	Notre Dame	57
68	Evansville	65
61	DePauw	62
85	Indiana State	88

9–17

The Hinkle Statistics

1967–68

57	Illinois	75
69	Northwestern	87
75	Oklahoma	79
58	Western Kentucky	76
65	Michigan State	55
73	Toledo	70
76	Purdue	59
69	Ohio State	71
76	Michigan	93
74	Murray State	86
65	Ball State	78
78	Valparaiso	63
70	St. Joseph's	87
64	Evansville	92
86	Indiana State	85
77	Notre Dame	82
101	St. Joseph's	61
62	Wabash	60
66	DePauw	68
74	Wabash	73
79	Valparaiso	76
89	Ball State	81
89	Evansville	82
68	DePauw	81
55	Indiana State	83

11–14

1968–69

66	Illinois	105
69	Northwestern	73
55	Purdue	93
60	Michigan State	70
67	Western Kentucky	65
71	Weber State	91
71	Ohio State	74
79	Michigan	101
81	New Mexico (OT)	80
64	Ball State	75
74	Indiana State	72
73	Notre Dame	76
68	Valparaiso	75
88	Evansville	85
86	DePauw	73
69	St. Joseph's	70
82	Wabash	71
95	Ball State	75
90	Indiana State	80
74	Wabash	59
80	Valparaiso	78
83	Evansville	96
90	Notre Dame	94
87	DePauw (OT)	94
87	St. Joseph's	81
68	Toledo	96

11–15

1969–70

67	Illinois	83	94	Evansville	88
89	Ohio State	112	89	DePauw	90
64	Purdue	100	103	St. Joseph's	90
61	Western Kentucky	96	108	Oral Roberts	96
85	Idaho State	69	102	Ball State	95
81	Michigan State	60	91	Indiana State	93
73	Toledo	74	106	Wabash	91
72	Murray State	69	99	Valparaiso	87
92	Pepperdine	85	99	Evansville	87
65	Michigan	105	111	DePauw	86
88	Ball State	82	77	St. Joseph's	79
100	Indiana State (OT)	104	114	Notre Dame	121
95	Valparaiso	80			
88	Wabash	71	15–11		

HINKLE-BUTLER BASKETBALL RECORD AGAINST MAJOR OPPONENTS

	W	L
Ball State	37	11
Bradley	3	6
Chicago	4	1
Cincinnati	5	3
City College of New York	1	3
Dartmouth	2	0
DePauw	54	16
Evansville	27	23
Franklin	27	6
Illinois	6	23
Indiana Central	4	4
Indiana State	28	21
Indiana	5	16
Iowa	5	3
Long Island	1	2
Louisville	3	2
Loyola	4	2
Marquette	8	6
Miami (Ohio)	5	1
Michigan	12	15
Michigan State	10	11
Northwestern	5	11
Notre Dame	18	58
Ohio State	6	21
Pittsburgh	7	5
Princeton	2	0
Purdue	13	19
Southern California	2	2
St. Joseph's	32	11
Toledo	4	5
UCLA	1	4
Valparaiso	35	13
Wabash	66	16
Western Kentucky	2	3
Wisconsin	9	12
Yale	2	0

HINKLE–GREAT LAKES NAVAL TRAINING CENTER BASKETBALL SEASONS

1942–43

55	Milwaukee Teachers	36
73	St. Norbert	24
70	DePauw	36
49	Ohio State	46
76	Lawrence	43
53	Illinois	57
55	Glenview Air Base	32
82	Fort Sheridan	33
59	Butler	34
57	Stanford	41
47	Northwestern	59
48	Purdue	43
63	St. Norbert	21
38	Michigan State	34
60	St. Joseph's (Indiana)	32
60	Marquette	54
63	Creighton	55
64	Chicago	35
61	Wisconsin	43
92	Missouri	45
47	Kansas	41
63	St. Joseph's (Indiana)	28
34	Detroit	30
68	Carroll	32
55	Wisconsin	48
57	Northwestern	36
68	Lake Forest	33
79	Calvin	44
60	Purdue	38
51	Washington (St. Louis)	33
60	Notre Dame	56
56	Marquette	37
56	Michigan State	39
46	Minnesota (OT)	41
53	Kentucky	39
42	Notre Dame (OT)	44

33–3

1943–44

64	Glenview Naval Air Station	38
86	Chicago	29
52	Illinois	44
65	Bowling Green	41
58	Purdue	52
59	Minnesota	32
45	DePauw	26
51	Illinois	64
36	Northwestern	54
52	Ohio State	46
76	Fort Sheridan	52
71	Western Michigan	40
59	Lawrence	27
83	Illinois Normal	53
63	Fort Custer	38
45	Marquette	36
57	Glenview Naval Air Station	41
72	Ottumwa Naval Air Station	30
46	Northwestern	36
58	Western Michigan	43
55	Toledo	25
85	Illinois Normal	47
67	Marquette	24
44	Bowling Green	37
50	Lawrence	35
63	Wisconsin	40
84	Notre Dame	48
60	Purdue	46
54	DePauw	35
51	Notre Dame	54
55	Phillips 66 Oilers	39
77	Toledo	29
52	St. Thomas (St. Paul)	35
63	Wisconsin	47

31–3

HINKLE BASKETBALL LETTERMEN WHO COACHED HIGH SCHOOL OR COLLEGE TEAMS

(C) denotes a team captain; (M) denotes a manager

Allen, Wilbur 1928–30
Armstrong, Scott 1934–36
Baird, Frank 1932–34 (C)
Baker, Dee 1949–50
Batts, Roscoe 1934–36
Bevelhimer, Paul 1951
Blackwell, Jess 1961
Bose, Orville 1959–60
Braden, Carl 1942–43
Braun, Leo 1961–62
Bugg, William 1927–29
Bultman, Erv 1962
Burdsall, Orvis 1950–52 (C)
Butcher, Gary 1963–65 (M)
Caskey, Jake 1929
Cave, Marvin 1948
Chadd, Archie 1926–28 (C)*
Chickedantz, Harry 1931–33
Clark, Ed 1966–67 (M)
Cook, Art 1945–46 (C)
Cosgrove, Art 1935–38 (C)
Cox, Wally 1955–58
Craft, Ray 1958
Crosley, Jim 1952–54 (C)
Deputy, Jim 1941–42
Dietz, Bob 1939–41 (C)
Doyle, Jim 1947–50
Ellenberger, Norm 1953–54
Engle, Earl 1959, 1962
Evans, Bob 1947–49
Ferrin, Gregg 1963–64
Fields, Walter 1949
Fine, Marion 1946
Floyd, Walter 1927–28
Geyer, William 1937–39
Greve, Keith 1952–54, 1958 (C)
Gunn, Byron 1939–40
Guzek, Ted 1955–58
Haffner, Dick 1959–60
Harper, Clarence 1968–69
Haslam, Dick 1960–62
Heddon, Frank 1931 (M)
Hohlt, Jim 1967
Holloway, Don 1952–53, 1955 (C)
Howell, Jim 1954
Iwema, Ron 1963–65
Jones, Troy 1934–36 (C)
Joseph, Loren 1939–40
Jung, Phil 1957
Leffler, Mike 1958–59
Maas, Charles 1947–49 (C)
Marsh, John 1970
McCray, James 1940–41
Mehl, Bob 1949
Milner, Gene 1966–67
Moses, John 1959
Neat, Lyle 1939–41
Neat, Scott 1969
Norris, Steve 1968–70
O'Brien, Walter 1950
Overman, Earl 1935, 1937
Pearson, Joe 1970
Pennington, Ken 1958–60 (C)
Peterman, Mark 1955–57 (C)
Petty, Jerry 1960
Petty, Jim 1966
Poland, Laural 1937–39
Pope, Gordon 1962–63
Porter, Harry 1953–54
Proffitt, Searle 1931–33 (C)

Ramey, Larry 1959–61
Reynolds, Cleon 1929–30
Riley, Ray 1957
Rosenstihl, Jim 1951
Schilling, Ed 1966–67 (C)
Schwomeyer, Herbert 1942
Scott, Bill 1958–59 (C)
Shepherd, William, Sr. 1947–49
Shook, Larry 1962–63
Steiner, Jerry 1938–40 (C)
Theofanis, George 1952, 1957
Tidrow, Ernie 1942–43
Toon, Herod 1945–48 (C)
Vandermeer, Melvin 1939–40
Wood, Marvin 1948–50**

*Anderson High School State Champions 1935, 1937
**Milan High School State Champions 1954

HINKLE-BUTLER BASEBALL

	W	L	T
1921	4	5	
1922	11	4	
1923	3	4	
1924	13	9	
1925	14	7	
1926	9	6	
1927	3	3	
1933	3	4	
1934	3	7	1
1935	2	5	
1936	7	10	
1937	5	12	
1938	12	4	
1939	10	7	
1940	7	7	
1941	7	7	
1946	6	6	
1947	9	6	
1948	11	7	
1949	10	5	
1950	9	10	
1951	10	7	
1952	8	8	
1953	10	8	
1954	11	8	
1955	5	11	1
1956	7	9	
1957	11	5	1
1958	9	9	
1959	10	6	
1960	6	9	
1961	5	10	
1962	9	6	
1963	11	8	
1964	7	9	
1965	9	10	
1966	6	9	
1967	9	13	
1968	9	8	1
1969	12	5	
1970	3	12	
Totals	325	305	4

HINKLE BASEBALL LETTERMEN WHO COACHED HIGH SCHOOL OR COLLEGE TEAMS

(C) denotes a team captain

Athnan, Rex 1957–58
Bain, Paul 1947–48
Baird, Frank 1932–34
Baker, Dee 1948–50
Batts, Roscoe 1934–35
Blackburn, George 1946, 1948–49
Boa, Andy 1936, 1938
Braden, Harold 1939
Bradford, Jack 1947–48
Broderick, Bernie 1941–42
Burdette, Cody 1936, 1938
Butler, George 1942, 1948
Campbell, Dick 1951–52, 1954 (C)
Campbell, Don 1950–52
Caporale, Egidio 1960
Chickedantz, Harry 1933
Compton, Leroy (Dee) 1945–47
Cook, Arthur 1945, 1947
Craig, Kenneth 1968, 1970
Craver, Jim 1967–69
Diederich, Ed 1921–22
Donna, Gary 1964–66
Doyle, James 1947–50
Dunker, Don 1967–68
Ellenberger, Norm 1951–52
Enright, Dave 1964–65
Fields, Walter 1947–49 (C)
Fisher, Charles 1935
Fisher, Glenn 1942, 1946
Fisher, Ralph 1950
Freeman, Ken 1962–63
Gantz, Steve 1967–68
Greve, Keith 1954
Guleff, Methody 1939–41
Haffner, Dick 1959–60
Harding, Tom 1938
Howell, Jim 1954
Hudson, Bill 1950–52
Hunckler, Fred 1941–43
Iwema, Ron 1963–65
Johnson, Charles 1952
Kokinda, John 1968
Kouns, Beryl 1954–55
Kurth, Richard 1968–71
Laymon, Clarence 1935–36 (C)
LeBeau, Craig 1969–70
Leffler, Mike 1959
Levenhagen, Fred 1966–67
Long, Ken 1959
Maas, Charles 1947–49
Macek, Joe 1936, 1938
Males, John 1949–50
Manifold, Howard 1946
Manifold, Lothair 1946
Manifold, Walter 1947
Masariu, John 1946
Melson, Frank 1946
Middlesworth, Hugh W. 1921–24 (C)
Moses, John 1957–59
Neat, Lyle 1939–41
Neat, Scott 1968–69
Neely, Jeff 1968–69, 1971
Pearson, Joe 1970
Petty, Glenn 1961, 1963
Renie, Tim 1961–63
Renie, Tom 1963–64
Riley, Ray 1957

Rosenstihl, James 1948–51 (C)
Schumacher, Max 1954
Shepherd, William 1948–49
Shook, Larry 1961–63
Steiner, Jerome 1938–40
Strafford, Bill 1959–61
Sutphin, Karl 1933–35
Tex, Guy 1940–41, 1946 (C)
Toon, Herod, Jr. 1945–48
Wiley, Thomas 1948
Wilhoite, Maurice 1950, 1952
Wolf, Hugh 1952

INDEX

Index

Index

Index

Index

Index

Index

Index

Index

Index

HOWARD CALDWELL is one of the best-known and most highly respected television newscasters in Indiana. Anchor of the WRTV Channel 6 early evening news since 1959, he has also been anchor of the late news (1960–66 and 1973–87). Before coming to WRTV, he worked in print journalism and radio. He has also produced the popular series of feature stories about the state entitled "Howard's Indiana." Caldwell has received numerous awards for his reporting as well as community activities. In 1984 he was awarded an honorary doctorate from Butler University.